AMERICAN POLITICAL, ECONOMIC, AND SECURITY ISSUES

FEDERAL REGULATORY COSTS

ESTIMATES AND ANALYSIS

AMERICAN POLITICAL, ECONOMIC, AND SECURITY ISSUES

Additional books in this series can be found on Nova's website under the Series tab.

Additional E-books in this series can be found on Nova's website under the E-books tab.

ECONOMIC ISSUES, PROBLEMS AND PERSPECTIVES

Additional books in this series can be found on Nova's website under the Series tab.

Additional E-books in this series can be found on Nova's website under the E-books tab.

AMERICAN POLITICAL, ECONOMIC, AND SECURITY ISSUES

FEDERAL REGULATORY COSTS

ESTIMATES AND ANALYSIS

RICHARD N. MARAPAO
AND
CATHERINE G. ABULOG
EDITORS

Nova Science Publishers, Inc.
New York

For permission to use material from this book please contact us:
Telephone 631-231-7269; Fax 631-231-8175
Web Site: http://www.novapublishers.com

Library of Congress Cataloging-in-Publication Data

Federal regulatory costs : estimates and analysis / editors, Richard N. Marapao and Catherine G. Abulog.
p. cm.
Includes bibliographical references and index.
ISBN 978-1-61470-389-1 (hbk. : alk. paper) 1. Trade regulation--United States--Costs. 2. Trade regulation--United States--Cost effectiveness. I. Marapao, Richard N. II. Abulog, Catherine G.
HD3616.U47F37 2011
338.5'1--dc23

2011023221

Published by Nova Science Publishers, Inc. † New York

CONTENTS

PREFACE

Regulation, like taxing and spending, is a basic function of government. Each year federal agencies issue between 3,000 and 4,000 final rules on topics ranging from the timing of bridge openings to the permissible levels of arsenic and other contaminants in drinking water. Unlike taxing and spending, however, the costs that nonfederal entities pay to comply with federal regulations are not accounted for in the federal budget process. Some policy makers have expressed an interest in measuring total regulatory costs and benefits. However, measuring total regulatory costs and benefits is inherently difficult. This book provides an analysis of the estimate of total costs of federal regulation with a focus on the regulatory costs on small firms.

Chapter 1- Some policy makers have expressed an interest in measuring total regulatory costs and benefits (e.g., the Congressional Office of Regulatory Analysis Creation and Sunset and Review Act of 2011, H.R. 214, 112th Congress), and estimates of total regulatory costs have been cited in support of regulatory reform legislation (e.g., H.R. 10, the Regulations from the Executive In Need of Scrutiny (REINS) Act, H.R. 10, 112th Congress). However, measuring total costs and benefits is inherently difficult. This report examines one such study to illustrate the complexities of this type of analysis.

Chapter 2- The annual cost of federal regulations in the United States increased to more than $1.75 trillion in 2008. Had every U.S. household paid an equal share of the federal regulatory burden, each would have owed $15,586 in 2008. By comparison, the federal regulatory burden exceeds by 50 percent private spending on health care, which equaled $10,500 per household in 2008. While all citizens and businesses pay some portion of these costs, the distribution of the burden of regulations is quite uneven. The portion of regulatory costs that falls initially on businesses was $8,086 per employee in 2008. Small businesses, defined as firms employing fewer than 20 employees, bear the largest burden of federal regulations. As of 2008, small businesses face an annual regulatory cost of $10,585 per employee, which is 36 percent higher than the regulatory cost facing large firms (defined as firms with 500 or more employees).

In: Federal Regulatory Costs
Editors: R. N. Marapao, C. G. Abulog
ISBN: 978-1-61470-389-1

Chapter 1

ANALYSIS OF AN ESTIMATE OF THE TOTAL COSTS OF FEDERAL REGULATIONS*

Curtis W. Copeland

SUMMARY

Some policy makers have expressed an interest in measuring total regulatory costs and benefits (e.g., the Congressional Office of Regulatory Analysis Creation and Sunset and Review Act of 2011, H.R. 214, 112th Congress), and estimates of total regulatory costs have been cited in support of regulatory reform legislation (e.g., H.R. 10, the Regulations from the Executive In Need of Scrutiny (REINS) Act, H.R. 10, 112th Congress). However, measuring total costs and benefits is inherently difficult. This report examines one such study to illustrate the complexities of this type of analysis.

A September 2010 report prepared by Nicole V. Crain and W. Mark Crain for the Office of Advocacy within the Small Business Administration (SBA) stated that the annual cost of federal regulations was about $1.75 trillion in 2008. This cost estimate was developed by adding together the estimated costs of four categories or types of regulation: economic regulations (estimated at $1.236 trillion); environmental regulations ($281 billion); tax compliance ($160 billion);

* This is an edited, reformatted and augmented version of a Congressional Research Service 7-5700, R41763 publication, prepared for Members and Committees of Congress dated April 6, 2011.

and regulations involving occupational safety and health, and homeland security ($75 billion). Some commenters have raised questions about the validity and reliability of this estimate.

For example, Crain and Crain's estimate for economic regulations (which comprises more than 70% of the $1.75 trillion estimate) was developed by using an index of "regulatory quality." One of the authors of the regulatory quality index said that Crain and Crain misinterpreted and misused the index, resulting in an erroneous and overstated cost estimate. Other commenters have also raised concerns about using the index to estimate regulatory costs, and about the regression analysis that the authors used to produce the cost estimate. Crain and Crain said that they believe they interpreted and used the regulatory quality index correctly.

Crain and Crain's estimates for environmental, occupational safety and health, and homeland security regulations were developed by blending together academic studies (some of which are now more than 30 years old) with agencies' estimates of regulatory costs that were developed before the rules were issued (some of which are now 20 years old). Although the agency estimates were typically presented as low-to-high ranges, Crain and Crain used only the highest cost estimates in their report. The Office of Management and Budget has said that estimates of the costs and benefits of regulations issued more than 10 years earlier are of "questionable relevance."

Crain and Crain's estimate for the cost of tax paperwork was based on data from the Internal Revenue Service and the Tax Foundation, but OMB data indicate that the number of hours of tax paperwork may be much higher than Crain and Crain's estimate. On the other hand, the authors' assumptions regarding the cost of completing the paperwork may be too high. A threshold question, however, is whether tax paperwork should be considered in the same category as regulatory costs. OMB does not include tax paperwork in its annual reports to Congress.

Crain and Crain said they did not provide estimates of the benefits of regulations, even when the information was readily available, because the SBA Office of Advocacy did not ask them to do so. OMB's reports to Congress have generally indicated that regulatory benefits exceed costs. Crain and Crain said their report was not meant to be a decision-making tool for lawmakers or federal regulatory agencies to use in choosing the "right" level of regulation. This report will not be updated.

INTRODUCTION

Regulation, like taxing and spending, is a basic function of government. Each year, federal agencies issue between 3,000 and 4,000 final rules on topics ranging from the timing of bridge openings to the permissible levels of arsenic and other contaminants in drinking water. Unlike taxing and spending, however, the costs that nonfederal entities pay to comply with federal regulations are not accounted for in the federal budget process. Some policy makers have expressed an interest in measuring total regulatory costs and benefits. For example, the Congressional Office of Regulatory Analysis Creation and Sunset and Review Act of 2011 (H.R. 214, 112th Congress) would require the newly created office to issue "an annual report including estimates of the total costs and benefits of all existing Federal regulations." As discussed later in this report, for nearly 14 years, Congress has required the Office of Management and Budget (OMB) to prepare a report each year on the aggregate costs and benefits of federal rules.[1]

However, measuring total regulatory costs and benefits is inherently difficult. For example, researchers must determine the baseline for measurement (i.e., what effects would have occurred in the absence of the regulation) and aggregating the results of studies conducted years earlier with different methodologies and quality can be highly problematic. Some observers, including OMB, currently doubt whether an accurate measure of total regulatory costs and benefits is possible.

The Crain and Crain Report

In September 2010, the Office of Advocacy within the Small Business Administration (SBA) released a report prepared for the office by Nicole V. Crain and W. Mark Crain entitled "The Impact of Regulatory Costs on Small Firms."[2] Among other things, the report stated that the annual cost of federal regulations in 2008 was about $1.75 trillion. The September 2010 report was the fourth such report prepared for the SBA Office of Advocacy in the previous 15 years:

- In 1995, Thomas D. Hopkins estimated annual federal regulatory costs that year to be between $416 billion and $668 billion.[3]
- In 2001, W. Mark Crain and Hopkins estimated the annual cost of regulations in the year 2000 at $843 billion.[4]
- In 2005, W. Mark Crain estimated annual regulatory costs in 2004 at about $1.1 trillion.[5]

The $1.75 trillion estimate of regulatory costs has been widely quoted in the press,[6] by witnesses at congressional hearings,[7] and by Members of Congress,[8] and it has been cited as evidence of the need for regulatory reform legislation and congressional oversight actions.[9] Other observers, however, have criticized the estimate, saying that it overstates the total cost of federal regulations.[10]

This report examines how Crain and Crain developed the $1.75 trillion estimate of federal regulatory costs in 2008. It also compares the $1.75 trillion estimate for 2008 with the $1.1 trillion estimate for 2004, and with OMB's estimates of regulatory costs in 2008.

How Crain and Crain Developed the $1.75 Trillion Estimate of Regulatory Costs

- Crain and Crain developed their $1.75 trillion estimate of total regulatory costs by adding together cost estimates for each of four categories or types of regulation: economic regulations ($1.236 trillion); environmental regulations ($281 billion); tax compliance ($160 billion); and regulations involving occupational safety and health, and homeland security ($75 billion). As Figure 1 below illustrates, the estimated cost of economic regulations was more than 70% of the authors' estimate of total regulatory costs.

Economic Regulations

According to the Crain and Crain report, "[e]conomic regulations include a wide range of restrictions and incentives that affect the way businesses operate—what products and services they produce, how and when they produce them, and how products and services are priced and marketed to consumers."[11]

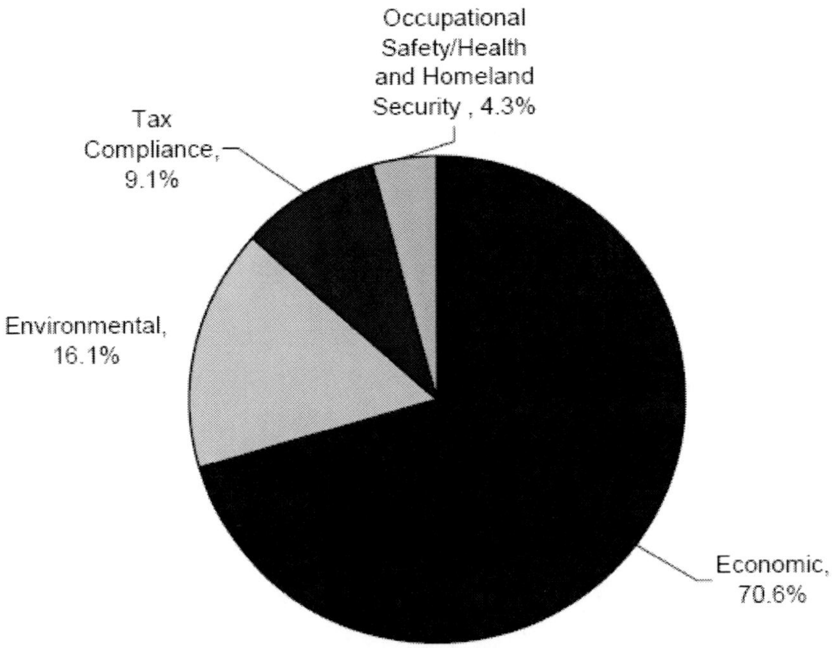

Source: CRS, based on data from Crain and Crain, September 2010.
Note: Due to rounding, the individual segments total 100.1%.

Figure 1. Economic Regulations Were More Than 70% of Crain and Crain's Estimate of Total Regulatory Costs.

They said such regulations affect both domestic and international business operations, and include quotas and tariffs on foreign imports that "limit competition from outside the United States, restrict production and employment, raise prices, and generally curtail U.S. economic activities."[12] To develop an estimate of the cost of economic regulations, Crain and Crain used a Worldwide Governance Index (WGI) of "regulatory quality" that was developed by Aart Kraay and Massimo Mastruzzi of the World Bank, and Daniel Kaufmann of the Brookings Institution.[13] According to Crain and Crain, the WGI regulatory quality index "measures perceptions of the ability of governments to formulate and implement sound policies and regulations that permit and promote private sector development."[14] Crain and Crain said the index was calibrated to range between -2.5 and +2.5, and that +2.5 represented "the minimal amount of regulation."[15] In 2008, the WGI regulatory quality index score for the United States was +1.579.

Crain and Crain used regression analysis[16] in an effort to determine the impact of changes in the regulatory quality index on real Gross Domestic Product (GDP) per capita, holding constant four other variables that they said the literature suggests explain differences in economic development across countries and over time: country population, primary education as a share of the eligible population, foreign trade as a share of GDP, and fixed broadband subscribers per 100 people. Using this approach, Crain and Crain concluded that a one-unit change in the WGI regulatory quality index (e.g., a change from +1.5 to +2.5 on the scale) represented a 9.4% change in real GDP per capita. Because the regulatory quality index for the United States in 2008 was +1.579, Crain and Crain said that the 0.921 difference between that value and the +2.5 maximum represented an 8.7% reduction in GDP (0.094 times 0.921) because of economic regulations. Because GDP in the United States was about $14.2 trillion in 2008, Crain and Crain concluded that the types of economic regulations included in the regulatory quality index reduced real GDP per capita in the United States by about $1.236 trillion ($14.2 trillion times 0.087).[17]

Composition of the Regulatory Quality Index

According to Kaufmann, Kraay, and Mastruzzi, the WGI index of regulatory quality for the United States in 2008 was determined by aggregating six expert-based measures and two surveys, each of which was scored on a 0 to 1 scale.[18] The six expert-based measures, their scores, and the particular factors considered in each measure were as follows:

- Economist Intelligence Unit (scored at 0.70), a commercial business information provider headquartered in London, England. The score is based on its experts' judgment of 16 factors, including "protectionism in the country negatively affects the conduct of business," "access to capital markets (foreign and domestic) is easily available," "real corporate taxes are non distortionary," "labor regulations hinder business activities," and "easy to start a business."
- Global Insight Business Conditions and Risk Indicators (scored at 0.94). Global Insight is a commercial business information provider headquartered in Boston, Massachusetts. The score is based on its experts' assessment of two factors: (1) "tax effectiveness," defined as "how efficient the country's tax collection system is"; and (2)

"legislation," defined as "whether the necessary business laws are in place, and whether there any outstanding gaps."

- Global Insight Global Risk Service (scored at 0.95). Global Risk Service is a commercial business information provider headquartered in Boston, Massachusetts. The score is based on its experts' judgment of five factors: (1) "export regulation," (2) "import regulation," (3) "other business regulation," (4) "nonresident business ownership restrictions," and (5) "nonresident equity ownership restrictions."
- Heritage Foundation Index of Economic Freedom (scored at 0.73). The Heritage Foundation is described by the WGI index as a "nongovernmental research and educational institute headquartered in Washington, United States, advocating conservative public policies." The index score is based on its experts' judgment of two factors: (1) "foreign investment" and "banking/finance."
- Institutional Profiles Database (scored at 0.89), which is provided by the French government's Ministry of the Economy. The score is based on its experts' judgment of four factors: (1) "ease of starting a business," (2) "administered prices and market prices," (3) "competition: productive sector: ease of market entry for new firms," and (4) "competition between businesses: competition regulation arrangements."
- Political Risk Services International Country Risk Guide (scored at 1.00). Political Risk Services is a commercial business information provider headquartered in Syracuse, New York. The score is based on their experts' judgment of one factor entitled "investment profile," summarizing the investment environment.

The two surveys used to develop the regulatory quality index, their values, and the particular factors considered in each survey were as follows:

- Institute for Management and Development World Competitiveness Yearbook (scored at 0.50). The Institute for Management Development is an educational and research organization headquartered in Lausanne, Switzerland. The score is based on a survey of business people working in the United States, who are asked to comment on the same 16 factors used by the Economist Intelligence Unit mentioned above (e.g., "protectionism in the country negatively affects the conduct of business," "access to capital markets (foreign and domestic) is easily available," "real corporate taxes are non distortionary," "labor regulations hinder business activities," and "easy to start a business").

- World Economic Forum Global Competitiveness Report (scored at 0.62). The World Economic Forum is an international organization based in Switzerland. Its survey asked domestic and foreign-owned firms their views regarding seven statements: (1) "administrative regulations are burdensome," (2) "tax system is distortionary," (3) "import barriers/cost of tariffs as obstacle to growth," (4) "competition in local market is limited," (5) "it is easy to start company," (6) "anti-monopoly policy is lax and ineffective," and (7) "environmental regulations hurt competitiveness."

Some observers have questioned whether WGI indices, such as the regulatory quality index, "measure what they purport to measure,"[19] and the authors of the WGI have responded to those concerns.[20] Crain and Crain noted in their report that the World Bank Development Research Group published a detailed description of how the WGI indices were developed,[21] and noted that the WGI indices were correlated with an index of economic regulations developed by the Organization for Economic Cooperation and Development (OECD) that Crain had used in his 2005 study of federal regulatory costs.[22] Crain and Crain said they used the WGI regulatory quality index in their 2010 study because it covered more countries for a longer period of time than the OECD index, and because it used a variety of sources and dimensions.

In a "Frequently Asked Questions" page on the World Bank's website, the WGI authors indicated that indices such as the regulatory quality index are "useful as a first tool for broad cross-country comparisons and for evaluating broad trends over time," but cautioned that they are "often too blunt a tool to be useful in formulating specific governance reforms in particular country contexts." They went on to say that such reforms "need to be informed by much more detailed and country-specific diagnostic data that can identify the relevant constraints on governance in particular country circumstances."[23]

Comments Regarding the Estimate of the Cost of Economic Regulations

The validity and accuracy of Crain and Crain's estimate of the cost of economic regulations depends on at least two factors: (1) whether the WGI index of "regulatory quality" can be used as part of a formula to measure the cost of economic regulations, and (2) whether the authors interpreted the regulatory quality index in the way it was intended. Several commenters on the Crain and Crain study have addressed one or both of these issues.

Comments from Aart Kraay of the World Bank

On January 27, 2011, Aart Kraay, a lead economist in the Development and Research Group at the World Bank, and one of the authors of the WGI regulatory quality index, contacted Crain and Crain by e-mail and provided his views on their use of the index in their September 2010 report on regulatory costs.[24] Kraay said that although "in principle an exercise like this could make sense," he said that he believed there were two "basic problems with how you use our data." First, he said that although Crain and Crain interpreted higher values of regulatory quality as "less stringent regulations," "[t]his isn't a good characterization of what the [regulatory quality, or RQ] index measures—rather RQ seeks to measure perceptions of the overall quality of the regulatory environment, which is very different from simply measuring whether it is 'stringent' or not." Kraay noted that the United States came in at about the 90th percentile of all countries in the world, and that countries like Finland and Sweden rank ahead of the United States on regulatory quality. "So by this standard," he said, "it is hard to say that the RQ measure 'rewards' deregulation." He also said that he and the other WGI authors had "indicated throughout that the WGI indicators are not literally true and have non-trivial margins of error, indicating that there is of course imprecision in how countries are ranked."[25]

The second major issue that Kraay noted was that Crain and Crain "may be misinterpreting the units of the WGI" by comparing the United States' score of +1.579 to +2.5—what the authors referred to in the report as "the minimal amount of regulation,"[26] and what Nicole V. Crain had referred to in a *Wall Street Journal* article as a "conceptual regulatory environment."[27] In his e-mail to the authors, Kraay said the following:

> You claim that 2.5 is the "best possible" score on the WGI. But this isn't really correct as the WGI are measured in units which don't have a fixed upper or lower boundary (technically the units are those of a standard normal random variable). It would make a lot more sense for you to compare the US score on RQ with that of a country whose regulatory environment you prefer, and then use that difference in score to calibrate the costs of regulations. So for example the highest numbers we see on WGI-RQ in 2009 are around 1.8 for countries like Singapore, followed closely by Denmark (!). The US comes in at around 1.4. So a more relevant comparison would be between the US

> and Denmark, rather than between the US and 2.5. This of course would mean that your estimated costs of regulation would be a lot smaller, since the distance between the US and Denmark is much smaller than the distance between the US and 2.5.[28]

(Kraay told CRS that the WGI authors periodically make minor revisions to WGI data for previous years, thus explaining the difference between the +1.579 regulatory quality index that Crain and Crain cited, and the "around 1.4" value that he noted in his e-mail to Crain and Crain.)[29] Using the same 2008 data that Crain and Crain used in their study, the nation with the highest regulatory quality index was Ireland, with a value of +1.915.[30] Subtracting the United States' regulatory index value from that of Ireland yields a difference of 0.336 (1.915 minus 1.579). As noted earlier, Crain and Crain used regression analysis to conclude that a one-unit change in the regulatory quality index represented a 9.4% change in real GDP per capita. If this measure is correct, the 0.336 difference between the Ireland and United States regulatory quality indices suggests a 3.16% reduction in GDP (0.094 times 0.336 equals 0.0316) in the United States compared with Ireland, the country with the least "stringent" regulatory climate. Therefore, the monetary "cost" of this GDP reduction would be about $448 billion (0.0316 times $14.2 trillion GDP in 2008), or about $788 billion less than the $1.236 trillion that Crain and Crain calculated. However, all of the above calculations assume that higher values on the regulatory quality index reflect "less stringent regulations," which Kraay indicated it does not.

Kraay also told CRS that he had concerns about the quality of Crain and Crain's regression analysis. He said "The problem is simply that high scores on regulatory quality are correlated with a lot of other good policies and institutions which also matter for GDP per capita. And so it is hard to sort out how much of the correlation between RQ and GDP per capita is due to the regulatory environment per se, and how much is due to other stuff."[31] He also said that "unless one can perfectly control for all these other factors (which is nearly impossible), the econometric estimates [that Crain and Crain] provide will reflect not just the effects of regulation on output, but also of all those other policies that are correlated with regulation."

When contacted by CRS for comment, Crain and Crain said that they understood Kraay's conceptual argument that the regulatory quality index might not reflect changes in the "stringency" of regulation, but they said that "the empirical evidence indicates that it does in practice." They said the index captures the extent of regulation from a variety of stakeholders' perceptions, and noted the nature of the questions used to construct the index (e.g., "How problematic are labor regulations for the growth of your business?" and "How problematic are customs and trade regulations for the growth of your business?"). Crain and Crain also said they did not compare the United States to another country (e.g., Denmark) because to estimate the cost of regulations to small and large businesses (what they contracted with SBA to do), they needed to estimate the total cost of all regulations. They also said they do not believe that they misinterpreted the WGI measure because the documentation provided by the WGI authors indicates that the index values range from about -2.5 to +2.5, and they selected +2.5 as the "best approximation of the regulatory environment that we were trying to capture in our estimate."[32]

Other Commenters

Before publishing the Crain and Crain report, the SBA Office of Advocacy had the study peer reviewed by two economists—Bob Litan of the Kauffman Foundation,[33] and Richard Williams of the Mercatus Center[34] at George Mason University.[35] Litan's complete comments were "I looked it over and it's terrific. Nothing to add." Williams's comments were more extensive. Overall, he said that the study was a "great project," and he hoped his comments would make it stronger. In relation to the estimate of the costs of economic regulations, he said the use of the index of regulatory quality was an "innovative idea," but said he was "concerned that the index may not measure what the authors say it measures, and even if it does, it may overstate the costs of regulation when used in conjunction with the other measures."[36] Among other things, he said that the study "might over-estimate the total costs of regulation because the effect of the Regulatory Quality Index on GDP may also capture some or all of the effects of environmental, workplace, security, and tax regulations." On the other hand, Williams also said that "there are reasons to believe that [the index] may underestimate costs."[37] He said some of the problems "could perhaps be solved simply with a better and more careful explanation of what the Regulatory Quality Index really measures. To guard against over-estimating costs, however, the authors would either need to control for the effects of other types of regulation on GDP, or refrain from adding some or all of the costs that are estimated via other methods."

In February 2011, the Center for Progressive Reform (CPR) issued a report criticizing the Crain and Crain study, and has requested that SBA's Office of Advocacy withdraw its sponsorship of the report.[38] In relation to the estimate of economic regulatory costs, CPR said (among other things) that (1) the WGI authors did not intend the regulatory quality index to be a proxy measure for regulatory burden, or as a tool for critiquing a particular country's regulatory stringency; (2) the lack of a clear definition of "economic regulations" raises the possibility that it includes other types of regulatory costs, which could lead to double counting; (3) the regression analysis used in the report assumes a simplistic relationship between regulatory "stringency" and GDP; and (4) the report gives the false impression that the index of regulatory quality in the United States is low, even though the United States ranked 11th out of more than 200 countries.[39]

CRS Analysis of Crain and Crain's Linear Regression[40]

The Crain and Crain report analyzed data for 25 OECD countries in order to assess the effect of economic regulation on GDP per capita, a common measure of the standard of living.[41]

Economists generally believe that a country's standard of living is affected by a variety of factors, including the availability of (1) land and natural resources, (2) labor and human capital, (3) capital and infrastructure, (4) the level of technology and sophistication of business practices, and (5) opportunities to trade with other countries.[42] Most economists also believe that government interventions in the economy (e.g., through taxes, spending, and regulation) can affect a country's standard of living.[43]

As noted previously in this report, Crain and Crain used linear regression analysis to examine the relationship between GDP per capita and the regulatory quality index, controlling for the effects of four other independent variables: country population; foreign trade as a share of GDP; primary education as a share of the eligible population; and fixed broadband subscribers per 100 people.[44] These four control variables may not capture all of the factors that affect GDP per capita, and other measures of those factors may be more appropriate. For example, "fixed broadband subscribers per 100 people" may or may not capture all aspects of capital investment, and may also partially reflect other factors (e.g., the state of information technology investment, population density, and per capita income levels).[45] The Crain and Crain report did not discuss how the authors selected the control variables used in their analysis.

Crain and Crain also used an estimation strategy that appears non-standard. Like many researchers, Crain and Crain analyze data for several countries over multiple years, known as a cross-country panel data set. Linear regressions on panel data often include country-specific control variables (fixed effects) to take into account national idiosyncrasies that do not vary over time and year-specific control variables to account for shocks that affected all countries in the sample in a given year.[46] Crain and Crain, however, reported that year-specific control variables that were estimated to be statistically insignificant in an unreported first-stage regression were then omitted from the reported second-stage regression results.[47] The statistical properties of this two-stage estimation strategy, which appears to be novel, has apparently not been explored in peer-reviewed journals.

CRS asked Crain and Crain to provide us with a copy of the data that they used in their study, but the authors did not do so. In an effort to assess the sensitivity of their results, CRS ran a linear regression using similar, but somewhat different, data and methods.[48] The results indicated that the regulatory quality index had no discernable independent effect on GDP per capita, suggesting that the analysis is highly sensitive to the choice of control variables and measures. *Appendix* of this report discusses this sensitivity analysis and the results in greater detail.

While most economists believe that economic regulation, like other forms of government intervention, can affect a country's standard of living, those effects may be too subtle for a seven-year cross-country panel to pick up. A country's regulatory environment may evolve slowly, and may interact with social and political conditions, other instruments of public policy such as taxation. Understanding the relationship between a measure of regulatory quality and GDP per capita (or other measures of economic well being) may require more focused empirical tools.

Environmental Regulations

Crain and Crain said they developed their cost estimates for environmental regulations by following the same basic approach as used by OMB in its annual reports to Congress. For environmental regulations issued through the first quarter of the year 2000, the authors used OMB's estimate of environmental costs from its 2001 report to Congress[49] (which was drawn in part from a study by Robert W. Hahn and John A. Hird),[50] which the authors converted into 2001 dollars.[51] For environmental regulations issued from April 1999 through September 2001, Crain and Crain used the estimate of the cost of major environmental rules from OMB's 2002 report.[52] For each subsequent fiscal year (October through September), the authors used estimates of the cost of major environmental rules from the subsequent OMB report. By adding together all of these cost estimates and converting the estimates from 2001 dollars to 2009 dollars, the authors concluded that environmental regulations cost between $175 billion and $280 billion in 2009. However, to develop the cumulative cost of all regulations, Crain and Crain used only the $280 billion estimate. The authors said their use of only the upper-end estimate "reflects a judgment that cost estimates are absent for important environmental regulations and that government agencies tend to be conservative in estimating regulatory costs."[53]

The data that Crain and Crain used to estimate the costs of environmental rules represent a mix of academic estimates of the cost of all rules prior to 1988, agency estimates of the costs of all rules issued between 1987 and the first quarter of 2000, and agency estimates of the costs of major rules (e.g., those with a $100 million or more annual impact on the economy) issued from April 1999 through September 2008. Therefore, the unit of analysis is not the same for all of the years (i.e., all rules prior to the year 2000 versus major rules starting in April 1999), and the methodologies differ (i.e., academic studies prior to 1988, and agencies' ex ante estimates of regulatory costs after 1988). In its 2000 report to Congress, OMB said that summarizing the total costs and benefits of regulations by adding together diverse sets of individual studies was an "inherently flawed approach" because the studies vary in quality and methodology, use differing assumptions, and seldom analyze the interaction effects among tens of thousands of regulations.[54]

Also, the time periods covered by the cost estimates that Crain and Crain used overlap in some years, raising the possibility of double counting. For example, both the Hahn and Hird estimate and the agency estimates cover rules that were issued in calendar year 1987. In addition, the baseline estimates of rules issued through the first quarter of 2000 overlap with the estimates for the period April 1, 1999, to September 30, 2001 (i.e., both cover the period April 1, 1999, through March 31, 2000).

In two of the one-year periods covered by the Crain and Crain analysis, the authors appear to have incorrectly recorded the information on environmental regulatory costs from the OMB reports:

- For the period October 2002 through September 2003, the authors said that OMB's estimate was $335 million (in 2001 dollars). Actually, OMB reported those costs as $360 million (in 2001 dollars).[55]
- For the period October 2003 through September 2004, the authors said that OMB's estimate was $3,840 million to $4,073 million (in

2001 dollars). Actually, OMB reported those costs as $3,060 million to $3,211 million (in 2001 dollars).[56]

Also, Crain and Crain did not report any of OMB's estimates of the benefits of environmental regulations. As discussed later in this report, the authors indicated that regulatory benefits were not included because they researched the topic as required by the Office of Advocacy.[57] *Table 1* below shows both the estimated costs and estimated benefits of environmental rules from OMB's reports. Overall and in eight of the nine time periods covered by the table, the average estimated benefits were higher than the average estimated costs. In six of the nine time periods covered by the table, the lowest estimated benefits were higher than the highest estimated costs.

Table 1. Estimates of Costs and Benefits of Environmental Rules in OMB Reports to Congress

Years Rules Were Issued	Estimated Costs (millions of 2001$)	Estimated Benefits (millions of 2001$)	Source
Through 03/31/2000	$108,359 to $191,887	$109,490 to $1,817,280	OMB, 2001, Table 2
04/01/1999 to 09/30/2001	$11,380 to $12,812	$25,338 to $56,141	OMB, 2002, Table 7
10/01/2001 to 09/30/2002	$192	$1,250 to $4,818	OMB, 2003, Table 1
10/01/2002 to 09/30/2003	$360	$204 to $355	OMB, 2004, Table 1
10/01/2003 to 09/30/2004	$3,060 to $3,211	$10,935 to $100,703	OMB, 2005, Table 1-3
10/01/2004 to 09/30/2005	$2,609 to $3,373	$14,512 to $161,708	OMB, 2006, Table 1-3
10/01/2005 to 09/30/2006	$2,720 to $2,965	$5,113 to $42,109	OMB, 2007, Table 1-3
10/01/2006 to 09/30/2007	$7,475 to $7,584	$21,143 to $170,391	OMB, 2008, Table 1-3
10/01/2007 to 09/30/2008	$7,591 to $8,780	$7,475 to $37,810	OMB, 2008, Table 1-3
Total	$143,746 to $228,274	$195,460 to $2,391,315	OMB, 2001 to 2008

Source: OMB's annual reports on the costs and benefits of regulations, available at http://www.whitehouse.gov/ omb/inforeg_regpol_reports_congress/.

Notes: The estimates of rules issued "Through 03/31/2000" includes all rules. All of the other time periods include only major rules.

The highest estimated benefits were lower than the lowest estimated costs in only one of the time periods (October 1, 2002, to September 30, 2003).

Comments Regarding the Estimate of the Cost of Environmental Regulations

Crain and Crain said their report "assumes that OMB's coverage of environmental regulations has been relatively complete."[58] Peer reviewer Richard Williams's only comment about the estimate of environmental regulatory cost was that this statement should be noted as an assumption.

As noted earlier, Crain and Crain said they used only OMB's upper estimate of environmental costs because they believed cost estimates were absent for some important environmental regulations, and "government agencies tend to be conservative in estimating regulatory costs."[59] The authors stated in a footnote that several regulatory experts have drawn a similar conclusion about OMB environmental cost estimates, but also noted that "considerable debate continues."[60] Crain and Crain cited studies indicating that government agencies systematically overestimate benefits and underestimate costs, but also cited one study by Winston Harrington and others that reportedly concluded that overestimation of unit costs occurs about as often as underestimation.[61]

In its analysis of the Crain and Crain report, the Center for Progressive Reform said that agencies' estimates of environmental costs tend to be too high, reflecting estimates provided to them by industry, whom CPR said have an incentive to overstate costs. CPR also said that industry cost estimates (and therefore the agency estimates) do not take into account technological innovations that reduce the cost of compliance. To support its position on this issue, CPR cited four studies indicating that agencies' initial cost estimates tended to be too high.[62] CPR also questioned Crain and Crain's use of the Hahn and Hird study to estimate the cost of environmental regulations prior to 1988, noting that the study was more than 20 years old, synthesized other estimates developed by a small group of economists, and some of those studies used data that are now more than 30 years old.

In responding to comments on one of its reports to Congress on the costs and benefits of regulations, OMB noted the "theory that agency estimates, upon which many but not all of our estimates are based, systematically understate costs and overstate benefits because agency self-interest lies in regulation." OMB went on to say the following:

Although this view of agency behavior enjoys widespread support among academics as a theoretical matter, there is little documentation available to support it—perhaps because there are several potentially offsetting factors. For example, much of the data that agencies use to make their estimates of costs comes from the regulated entities who generally have the opposite incentives—namely, they will likely overstate costs to help convince decision makers not to issue the regulation. Also, as noted in our report, competitive firms over time frequently find more cost-effective ways, including new technologies, to comply with regulations than had been envisioned ex ante. Some commenters pointed to a set of case studies that is about to be published to support this contention. On the other hand, there is a large body of literature that shows that agencies tend to overestimate the benefits of their programs because, over time, technological progress—in communications to energy exploration to infectious disease—has reduced the long run expected benefits of earlier regulations.[63]

Tax Compliance

To estimate the costs associated with complying with federal tax paperwork, Crain and Crain said they compiled data from the Internal Revenue Service (IRS), and in some cases the Tax Foundation,[64] on the amount of time required to complete each type of tax form, and the number of filings per form. The authors concluded that businesses, individuals, and nonprofits devoted about 4.3 billion burden hours to completing tax paperwork in 2008 (about 2.28 billion burden hours for business and about 2.02 billion burden hours for individuals and nonprofits). To monetize that burden, Crain and Crain estimated the cost of completing business paperwork at $49.77 per hour for businesses (which they said was the average hourly rate for "human resources professionals" in 2009 from the Bureau of Labor Statistics website) and $31.53 per hour for individuals and nonprofits (which they said was the average hourly rate for "accountants and auditors" in 2009), for a total cost of about $159.6 billion.

Crain and Crain did not indicate in their report how they "compiled" data from the IRS website and the Tax Foundation to arrive at the estimated 4.3 billion hours of tax paperwork in 2008. According to the Information Collection Budget that OMB develops annually, the government-wide paperwork burden in FY2008 was about 9.71 billion burden hours, of which the Department of the Treasury accounted for about 7.78 billion burden hours.[65] Although the Information Collection Budget did not separately identify the number of burden hours for the IRS, in May 2009, the IRS represented about 77.8% of the government-wide estimate, and about 99.5% of the Treasury estimate.[66] If those same ratios applied in 2008, IRS paperwork would have been about 7.5 billion burden hours—about 3.2 billion hours higher than in the Crain and Crain report.

Certain aspects of how Crain and Crain monetized IRS burden hours are also unclear. For example, it is unclear why the authors assumed that "human resources professionals" would be completing all business tax paperwork, that all individuals and nonprofits would have their returns prepared by "accountants and auditors," or where on the "Bureau of Labor Statistics website" the hourly rates for human resources professionals ($49.77 per hour) and accountants and auditors ($31.53) were derived. According to the Bureau of Labor Statistics' Occupational Employment Statistics, in May 2009, tax preparers received an average salary of $17.34 per hour (median salary was $14.45 per hour).[67] Even if one assumed that total compensation (including benefits and overhead) was one-third higher, the average compensation for tax preparers would still be just over $23 per hour ($17.34 times 1.33). Using this figure for all tax compliance may balance out those businesses and individuals who prepare their returns themselves and those who use more expensive preparers.[68] Therefore, multiplying 7.5 billion burden hours times $23 per hour yields a total cost of about $172.5 billion—about $12.9 billion higher than the Crain and Crain estimate.

A threshold issue, however, is whether tax paperwork should be included in estimates of regulatory costs at all. OMB does not include tax paperwork in its annual reports to Congress on the costs and benefits of federal regulations. In one of the first of those reports, OMB said that "filling out tax forms is not the result of 'regulations' but rather of the tax code itself, with most regulations merely providing interpretations and clarifications of tax law."[69] Also, in testimony before the House Committee on Government Reform in July 2003, John D. Graham, administrator of the Office of Information and Regulatory Affairs (OIRA) within OMB, said the following:

> To a greater extent than for other agencies and programs, IRS paperwork burden is driven by a statute (the Tax Code), and in particular the complexities of the Code. To ensure taxpayer compliance with our tax laws, IRS must collect a tremendous amount of information. This task is complicated by a massive, complex Tax Code that is subject to continuous revision. In the 15 years following the 1986 overhaul of the Code, Congress passed 84 tax laws. These laws required IRS to create and/or revise reporting and recordkeeping requirements, which in turn increased taxpayer burden.

> The Internal Revenue Service also had to make several changes to the 1040 schedules to implement the Economic Growth and Tax Relief Reconciliation Act of 2001. These statutorily driven revisions increased the burden on taxpayers by 47 million hours. Moreover, there are other factors totally outside the control of IRS—most notably increases in the number of tax filings due to economic and population growth over the years—that increase the aggregate IRS burden hours but not—and this is important—the average burden on individual taxpayers.[70]

Occupational Safety and Health and Homeland Security Regulations

Because the "economic regulations" category included many types of workplace regulations, Crain and Crain said that their final category of regulatory costs included only workplace regulations that deal with safety and health, primarily those issued by the Occupational Safety and Health Administration (OSHA) within the Department of Labor, as well as regulations related to homeland security. To estimate the cost of occupational safety and health regulations prior to 2001 (estimated at more than $64.3 billion in 2009 dollars), the authors used information from a 2005 study by Joseph M. Johnson that reportedly synthesized and evaluated other studies of workplace regulations.[71] Crain and Crain said they then added data from OMB's 2009 report to Congress on regulatory costs and benefits on (1) 2001 to 2008 occupational safety and health regulatory costs (estimated at $471 million in 2009 dollars), and (2) all homeland security costs through 2008 (estimated at about $10.4 billion in 2009 dollars). Adding these elements together, the authors concluded that the total cost for occupational safety and health and homeland security regulations in 2008 was about $75.2 billion.

Crain and Crain said they obtained the estimate for occupational safety and health regulatory costs between 2001 and 2008 from Table 1-2 in OMB's 2009 report to Congress. That table reports the estimated costs and benefits of major federal rules within selected programs from October 1, 1998, through September 30, 2008. One of the programs was labeled "Occupational Safety and Health Administration," with the costs associated with four rules estimated at between $362 million and $389 million (in 2001 dollars). Several of those years (October 1998 through December 2000) appear to overlap with estimates provided in Johnson's study of costs prior to 2001, raising the issue of possible double counting.[72] Also, converting the OMB estimate to 2009 dollars yields a range of $440 million to $471 million. Therefore, although the authors did not explicitly say so, it appears that Crain and Crain only used the upper-end of OMB's estimated cost range for these regulations (as they did for environmental regulations).

Crain and Crain said they obtained their estimate for homeland security costs from page 18 of OMB's 2009 report. There, OMB reported that since the Department of Homeland Security was created, "agencies have finalized 17 major homeland security regulations that impose a total annual cost on the economy of between $4.2 billion to $8.6 billion. Converting these estimated costs in 2001 dollars to 2009 dollars yields a range of $5.1 billion to $10.4 billion. Therefore, although they did not say so in their report, it appears that Crain and Crain again only used OMB's upper-end of the estimated cost range. As noted earlier in this report, the authors said that their use of the upper-end of OMB's estimates for environmental rules reflected a judgment that cost estimates were absent for important regulations and that government agencies tend to be conservative in estimating regulatory costs.[73] On the other hand, OMB has said that there is little evidence that agencies' cost estimates are too conservative.[74]

The Center for Progressive Reform's analysis of the Crain and Crain report stated that the cost estimates that the authors used for occupational safety and health costs (both the Joseph M. Johnson study and the agency estimates of costs before the rules are published) likely overstate true compliance costs because they are based on information provided by regulated industries. CPR also said that the Johnson study inflates OSHA's original cost estimates by multiplying them by 5.5, which was reportedly done to take into account non-major rules for which costs were not estimated, and for fines imposed for violations of OSHA standards. CPR said it saw no justification for counting such fines as "regulatory costs." "Under this logic," CPR said, "mass lawbreaking raises regulatory costs, enabling regulatory opponents to argue that we need to reduce regulations because of these regulatory costs."[75]

COMPARISON OF CRAIN AND CRAIN'S 2008 ESTIMATE TO CRAIN'S 2004 ESTIMATE

As noted previously and as shown below in *Table 2*, in 2005, W. Mark Crain estimated total federal regulatory costs in 2004 at about $1.11 trillion. In 2010, Crain and Crain estimated those costs in 2008 at about $1.75 trillion—an increase of about $639 billion (57.4%) in four years. Some of this increase is due to inflation,[76] but the authors said that the main reason for the increase was a change in the methodology used in developing their estimate of the cost of economic regulations.[77] As *Table 2* below indicates, were it not for the increase in the cost estimate for economic regulations, the total estimated cost of the three other types of regulations would have decreased by about $6 billion between 2004 and 2008.

Table 2. Changes in Estimates of the Costs of Federal Regulations: 2004 to 2008

Type of Regulation	2004	2008	Increase/Decrease (%)
Economic	$591 billion	$1,236 billion	$645 billion increase
			(+109.1%)
Environmental	$221 billion	$281 billion	$60 billion increase
			(+27.1%)
Workplace	$106 billion	$75 billion	$31 billion decrease
			(-29.2%)
Tax Compliance	$195 billion	$160 billion	$35 billion decrease
			(-17.9%)
Total	$1,113 billion	$1,752 billion	$639 billion increase (+57.4%)

Source: The 2004 data are from Crain (2005), and the 2008 data are from Crain and Crain (2010).

Notes: In Crain and Crain's 2010 report, "workplace" regulations were termed "occupational safety and health, and homeland security" regulations.

Comparison of Crain and Crain's 2008 Estimate to OMB's Estimates

For nearly 15 years, Congress has required OMB to submit annual reports on the costs and benefits of federal regulations. The first such requirement was in Section 645 of the Treasury, Postal Service and General Government Appropriations Act, 1997 (P.L. 104-208), which required the director of OMB to submit a report by September 30, 1997, that provided (among other things) "estimates of the total annual costs and benefits of federal regulatory programs, including quantitative and nonquantitative measures of regulatory costs and benefits." Similar requirements were contained in other appropriations bills in subsequent years.

In 2001, Section 624 of the Treasury and General Government Appropriations Act, 2001, (31 U.S.C. § 1105 note), sometimes known as the "Regulatory Right-to-Know Act," put in place a permanent requirement for an OMB report on regulatory costs and benefits. Specifically, it requires OMB to prepare and submit with the President's budget an "accounting statement and associated report" containing an estimate of the total costs and benefits (including quantifiable and nonquantifiable effects) of federal rules and paperwork, to the extent feasible, (1) in the aggregate, (2) by agency and agency program, and (3) by major rule. The accounting statement is also required to contain an analysis of the impacts of federal regulation on state, local, and tribal governments, small businesses, wages, and economic growth.

OMB's Early Estimates of Total Regulatory Costs and Benefits

For the first several years, OMB provided estimates of total regulatory costs and benefits, and those estimates (particularly the benefits estimates) varied substantially from year to year.

- In its 1997 report, OMB estimated total federal regulatory costs in 1997 at $279 billion, and estimated the benefits of federal regulations at $298 billion.[78]
- In its 1998 report, OMB estimated federal regulatory costs at between $170 billion and $230 billion (in 1996 dollars as of 1998), and estimated regulatory benefits at between $260 billion and $3.5 trillion.[79] The dramatic increase in the benefits estimate (by a factor of 12) was almost entirely due to the inclusion of an Environmental Protection Agency (EPA) estimate of the benefits associated with the Clean Air Act. Many observers had serious questions regarding the use of this EPA estimate, and EPA itself said it had only a small probability of being correct.
- In its 2000 and 2001 reports, OMB estimated the cost of all social regulations at between $146 billion and $229 billion (in 1996 dollars as of 1999), and estimated benefits at between $254 billion and nearly $1.8 trillion.[80] The nearly 50% drop in the upper-bound benefits estimate (from $3.5 trillion to $1.8 trillion) was primarily caused by a

significant drop in the previously mentioned EPA estimate of the benefits of the Clean Air Act (from $3.2 trillion to $1.45 trillion).

Each year, OMB presented its aggregate cost and benefit estimates with strong caveats. For example, in its first report in 1997, OMB said "it is extremely difficult, if not impossible, to estimate the actual total costs and benefits of all existing Federal regulations with any degree of precision."[81] The next year OMB said "there is not yet a professional consensus on methods that would permit a complete, consistent accounting of total costs and benefits of Federal regulation."[82] Some of the methodological problems that OMB pointed out in these and other reports included the following:

- The baseline for measurement is often not clear (i.e., what costs and benefits would have occurred in the absence of the regulation). Regulatory requirements sometimes become standard business practice (e.g., requirements to remove lead from gasoline or to put air bags in automobiles), so cost or benefit reductions would be unlikely to occur if the rules were eliminated entirely.
- It is difficult to attribute costs or benefits to federal regulations as opposed to state or local rules, voluntary standards organizations, insurance requirements, or the tort system.
- Technological change can make previous estimates of benefits and costs extremely inaccurate.
- Aggregating the results of different studies is highly problematic, as the studies vary in the quality, methodology, and types of regulatory impacts they include.[83]
- It is unclear which rules should be included in any tabulation of regulatory costs and benefits (e.g., "transfer" regulations such as crop subsidy payments).

In developing its estimates of total regulatory costs, OMB did not include "transfer" rules (which OMB said were about $140 billion in costs and benefits in 1997) because it considered them to be payments that reflect a redistribution of wealth rather than social costs to society as a whole. OMB also excluded the costs associated with filling out tax paperwork (which OMB estimated were about $140 billion in 1997) because it did not consider filling out income tax forms "regulations" in the traditional sense. Neither did it include estimates for rules published after 1987 for which agencies did not conduct cost-benefit analyses (e.g., rules with less than a $100 million impact on the economy).

OMB's Reports Since 2001

OMB's "Regulatory Right-to-Know Act" reports since 2001 have differed from the office's previous reports in that they have not presented cost or benefit estimates for all rules in existence. Instead, OMB has presented information for all regulations that it reviewed within a particular time-frame that (1) had costs or benefits of at least $100 million annually and (2) the costs and benefits had been monetized by either the rulemaking agency or OMB. Specifically:

- OMB's report for 2002 presented information on the costs and benefits of all regulations meeting those criteria that it reviewed for a six-and-one-half year period from April 1, 1995, to September 30, 2001. OMB said the total cost of those rules was about $50 billion to $53 billion (in 2001 dollars), and the benefits ranged from $48 billion to $101 billion.[84]
- In its 2003 report, OMB provided estimates of the costs and benefits of 107 regulations meeting the above criteria that it reviewed during the 10-year period from October 1992 through September 2002. OMB estimated that the total costs of these rules ranged from nearly $37 billion to nearly $43 billion (in 2001 dollars), with benefits ranging from $146 billion to $230 billion. OMB noted that four rules issued by EPA accounted for a substantial fraction of the aggregate benefits for all 107 rules.[85]

Each report since 2003 has provided information for rules meeting the above criteria during the previous 10 years. In its 2002 report, OMB said its decision to present data for only certain rules during a limited time-frame was driven by the inconsistent and increasingly aged nature of many of the studies used to develop aggregate estimates. OMB went on to say that "we do not believe that the estimates of the costs and benefits of regulations issued over ten years ago are reliable or very useful for informing current policy decisions."[86] Therefore, OMB said that "in keeping with the spirit of OMB's new information-quality guidelines, we have decided not to reproduce the aggregate estimates that were contained in Appendix C of the draft report."[87]

The report went on to say that the total costs and benefits of all federal rules then in effect "could easily be a factor of ten or more larger." In its 2003 report, OMB said that estimates prepared for rules adopted prior to the 10-year period "are of questionable relevance now."[88]

This point was elaborated by John D. Graham, former administrator of OIRA, in testimony before the House Committee on Government Reform in July 2003:

> The fact that attempts to estimate the aggregate costs of regulations have been made in the past, such as the Crain and Hopkins estimate of $843 billion..., is not an indication that such estimates are appropriate or accurate enough for regulatory accounting. Although the Crain and Hopkins estimate is the best available for its purpose, it is a rough indicator of regulatory activity, best viewed as an overall measure of the magnitude of the overall impact of regulatory activity on the macro economy. The estimate, which was produced in 2001 under contract for the Office of Advocacy of the Small Business Administration, is based on a previous estimate by Hopkins done in 1995, which itself was based on summary estimates done in 1991 and earlier, as far back as the 1970s. The underlying studies were mainly done by academics using a variety of techniques, some peer reviewed and some not. Most importantly, they were based on data collected ten, twenty, and even thirty years ago. Much has changed in those years and those estimates may no longer be sufficiently accurate or appropriate for an official accounting statement. Moreover, the cost estimates used in these aggregate estimates combine diverse types of regulations, including financial, communications, and environmental, some of which impose real costs and others that cause mainly transfers of income from one group to another. Information by agency and by program is spotty and benefit information is nonexistent. These estimates might not pass OMB's information quality guidelines. In particular, many of the studies they relied upon for these aggregate estimates are not sufficiently transparent about the data and methods to facilitate the reproducibility of the information by qualified third parties. That is why we have opted in the most recent Reports to Congress to report just the costs and benefits of major regulations prepared by agencies and reviewed by OMB over the last ten years.[89]

Later that year, testifying on the Paperwork and Regulatory Improvements Act of 2004 (H.R. 2432, 108th Congress), Graham said that requiring agencies to submit annual estimates of the cost and benefits of all their rules, and mandating preparation of a complete inventory of the costs and benefits of all federal rules and paperwork requirements, was "not workable."[90]

OMB's 2009 Report to Congress

OMB's 2009 report to Congress provided estimates of the total annual benefits and costs of 98 regulations reviewed by OMB during the 10-year period from October 1, 1998, to September 30, 2008. The 98 rules were those that (1) were estimated to generate benefits or costs of approximately $100 million in any one year; and (2) a substantial portion of the benefits and costs were quantified and monetized by the agency or, in some cases, monetized by OMB. As *Table 3* below shows, OMB said that the estimated costs of these rules ranged from nearly $51 billion to nearly $60 billion, and the benefits were estimated to be between about $126 billion and about $663 billion (in 2001 dollars). Because the estimates were provided for only 98 rules meeting the above criteria, and because not all benefits and costs for even those rules could be assessed, OMB noted that the estimates were "not a complete accounting of all of the benefits and costs of all regulations issued during this period."[91]

Table 3. Estimates of the Total Benefits and Costs of Major Rules by Agency: October 1, 1998 – September 30, 2008 (in millions of 2001 dollars)

Agency	Number of Rules	Benefits	Costs
Department of Agriculture	6	$906 – $1,315	$1,014 – $1,353
Department of Education	1	633 – 786	349 - 589
Department of Energy	6	4,954 – 5,391	3,067 – 3,118
Department of Health and Human Services	18	20,522 – 32,426	3,879 – 4,387
Department of Homeland Security	1	20 – 29	13 – 99
Department of Housing and Urban Development	1	190	150
Department of Justice	1	275	108 – 118
Department of Labor	6	481 – 1605	320 347
Department of Transportation	18	11,256 – 19,098	5,218 – 8,968
Environmental Protection Agency	40	87,042 – 601,469	36,853 – 40,851
Total	98	126,277 – 662,584	50,973 – 59,978

Source: OMB's 2009 Report to Congress, Table 1-1.

As in its previous reports, OMB said it presented information only for a 10-year period because "pre-regulation estimates prepared for rules adopted more than ten years ago are of questionable relevance today."[92] OMB also said the following:

> Aggregating benefit and cost estimates of individual regulations—to the extent they can be combined—provides significant insight about the effects of regulations. But the resulting estimates are neither precise nor complete. Individual regulatory impact analyses vary in rigor and rely on different assumptions, including baseline scenarios, methods, and data. Summing across estimates involves the aggregation of analytical results that are not strictly comparable. [93]

How OMB 's and Crain and Crain's Estimates Differ

It is difficult to compare OMB's estimates of regulatory costs and Crain and Crain's estimates because they were constructed in very different ways, and because the presentation categories were different (e.g., by agency in OMB's study, and by type of regulation in the Crain and Crain study). For several reasons, Crain and Crain's estimates of annual regulatory costs in 2008 were much larger than the estimates provided by OMB.

- Crain and Crain included estimates of costs associated with all rules for certain periods, and major rules for other periods. Their estimates attempt to measure the cumulative costs of all rules. OMB's estimates included only major rules that met certain criteria that had been issued during a 10-year period.
- Crain and Crain included estimates of the cost of "economic regulations," whereas OMB's estimate did not include economic regulations.[94]
- Crain and Crain included costs associated with tax paperwork, whereas OMB's estimate did not include tax paperwork.

CONCLUDING OBSERVATIONS

Although accurate measures of the costs and benefits of all federal rules would be useful, decision makers using studies of aggregate regulatory costs and benefits to guide public policy need to be aware of those studies' conceptual and methodological underpinnings. The validity and reliability of Crain and Crain's \$1.75 trillion estimate of total federal regulatory costs in 2008 depends on the validity and reliability of its individual elements. More than 70% of the overall estimate (\$1.236 trillion) is based on the WGI index of regulatory quality for the United States, with the authors determining the extent to which economic regulations reflected in that index reduces per capita real GDP in the United States. However, one of the authors of the regulatory quality index has said that Crain and Crain misinterpreted the index, and that higher values on the index cannot be interpreted as "less stringent regulations." Even if it could, he said that the index for the United States should be compared to a country with a preferable index, not to an idealized "best possible" score on the index. Comparing the United States' regulatory quality index in 2008 to the country with the highest index that year (Ireland) would have reduced Crain and Crain's estimate of the cost of economic regulations by nearly two-thirds. Other commenters (including one of the peer reviewers of the Crain and Crain study) raised similar concerns about whether the regulatory quality index could be used to measure the cost of economic regulations, and about the regression analysis used to produce the cost estimate. Responding to these criticisms, Crain and Crain said that they continue to believe that the regulatory quality index indicates the stringency of a country's economic regulations, and believe that it was appropriate for them to compare the index for the United States to a "conceptual regulatory environment" represented by a 2.5 score rather than to another country with a somewhat higher index score. The World Bank indicates on its website that measures like the regulatory quality index are "often too blunt a tool to be useful in formulating specific governance reforms in particular country contexts."

Crain and Crain's estimates for environmental, occupational safety and health, and homeland security regulations were developed by mixing together academic studies (some of which were more than 30 years old) with agencies' estimates of regulatory costs that were developed before the rules were issued (some of which are now 20 years old). OMB has said that adding together diverse sets of individual studies to develop a summary measure of regulatory costs is an "inherently flawed" approach. The agency estimates that Crain and Crain used were drawn from OMB reports to Congress on the estimated costs and benefits of regulations, which were typically presented as low-to-high ranges. However, Crain and Crain used only the highest cost estimates from these reports, stating that they did so because the OMB estimates did not cover all regulations, and because they believe "government agencies tend to be conservative in estimating regulatory costs." OMB has said that there is little documentation to support this view, and empirical studies of agencies' regulatory cost estimates have not resolved the issue. Also, OMB has concluded that estimates of the costs and benefits of regulations issued more than 10 years earlier are of "questionable relevance." Since 2003, OMB's annual "Regulatory Right-to-Know Act" reports to Congress have only included information on the costs and benefits of major rules issued during the previous 10 years. Although OMB has recognized that this approach understates total regulatory costs and benefits, OMB has said it does not believe older estimates are reliable or useful in informing policy decisions.

In one of its first reports to Congress on this issue, OMB also said that the incremental costs of regulations (i.e., over and above what businesses and individuals would have done in the absence of regulations) tend to decrease over time, as companies' business practices and consumers' expectations change.

> Thus, although the National Highway Traffic Safety Administration has significantly increased the safety of automobiles, it is not likely that if the agency's regulations were eliminated the automobile companies would discontinue the safety features that had been mandated. Consumers demand safer cars than they used to and automobile companies are concerned about product liability. This same phenomenon exists with the environment, although probably to a lesser extent. Environmentally responsible behavior has become good for the bottom line.... Over time, this "rising baseline" phenomenon reduces the true costs and benefits of health, safety, and environmental regulations. Estimates of the aggregate costs and benefits of regulation that include unadjusted estimates from aging studies are thus likely to be over estimates of the current costs and benefits of those regulations.[95]

OMB went on to say that "it does not seem implausible that, for environmental and other social regulations over ten years old, no more than half of compliance costs would likely be saved if these Federal regulations magically disappeared over night."[96]

Crain and Crain's estimate for the cost of tax paperwork was reportedly based on data from the IRS and the Tax Foundation, but data in OMB's annual Information Collection Budget suggests that the number of hours of tax paperwork may be much higher than the authors used in their report. On the other hand, Crain and Crain's assumptions regarding the per hour cost of completing the paperwork may be too high (e.g., the assumption that "human resources professionals" paid at nearly $50 per hour would be completing all business paperwork). However, a threshold question is whether tax paperwork should be considered in the same category as regulatory costs. OMB does not include tax paperwork in its annual reports to Congress on regulatory costs and benefits.

Regulatory Benefits

Although Crain and Crain attempted to determine all of the costs associated with federal regulations, their report did not discuss the benefits of those regulations—even when information on regulatory benefits was readily available in the OMB reports that they used to determine regulatory costs. In their report, the authors said that it "does not address the benefits of regulation, an important challenge that would be a logical next step toward achieving a rational regulatory system."[97] Crain and Crain told CRS that they did not include regulatory benefits in their study "because we researched the topic as required by the Office of Advocacy."[98] The SBA Office of Advocacy confirmed that Crain and Crain "were not asked to look at benefits, as the task for this last iteration was to update the previous study, which also looked at costs and the disproportionality between small and large businesses."[99]

Executive Order 12866 requires covered agencies to "assess both the costs and the benefits of the intended regulation and, recognizing that some costs and benefits are difficult to quantify, propose or adopt a regulation only upon a reasoned determination that the benefits of the intended regulation justify its costs."[100] It also says that agencies should generally select regulatory approaches that "maximize net benefits." OMB's reports to Congress on the aggregate costs and benefits of federal regulations have generally indicated that the estimated benefits exceed the estimated costs. For example, see the following:

- In the report for 2010 covering major rules reviewed by OMB from October 1999 through September 2009 for which benefits and costs were monetized, the aggregate costs were estimated to be between $43 billion and $55 billion, and the aggregate benefits were estimated to be between $128 billion and $616 billion. Of the 16 major rules issued during FY2009 for which benefits and costs were monetized, the costs were estimated at between $3.7 billion and $9.5 billion, and the benefits were estimated at between $8.6 billion and $28.9 billion.[101]

- In the draft report for 2011 covering major rules reviewed by OMB from October 2000 through September 2010 for which benefits and costs were monetized, the aggregate costs were estimated to be between $44 billion and $62 billion, and the aggregate benefits were estimated to be between $136 billion and $651 billion. Of the 18 major rules issued during FY2010 for which benefits and costs were monetized, the costs were estimated at between $6.5 billion and $12.5 billion, and the benefits were estimated at between $23.3 billion and $82.3 billion.[102]

Each year, however, there were a number of rules in which the agencies only quantified or monetized benefits or costs, but not both. Most commonly, the agencies quantified or monetized only costs.

Policymaking and the Crain and Crain Estimate

As noted at the beginning of this report, Crain and Crain's estimate that federal regulations cost $1.75 trillion in 2008 has been cited as evidence of the need for regulatory reform legislation. However, Crain and Crain told CRS that their report was "not meant to be a decision-making tool for lawmakers or federal regulatory agencies to use in choosing the 'right' level of regulation. In no place in any of the reports do we imply that our reports should be used for this purpose. (How could we recommend this use when we make no attempt to estimate the benefits?)"[103]

As Crain and Crain suggest, information on regulatory costs alone, whether for individual rules or for all rules in the aggregate, provides only one piece of information that Congress and other policymakers can use in determining how to proceed. For example, even if all federal regulations did cost $1.75 trillion in 2008 (which at least some commenters believe may not be correct), if the monetized benefits of those regulations were determined to be greater than those costs, then policymakers may conclude that those costs were (in the words of Executive Order 12866) "justified." On the other hand, if the monetized benefits of federal regulations were estimated to be less than the estimated costs, policymakers may reach another conclusion, or may decide to examine any non-monetized costs and benefits of those rules. But a valid, reasoned policy decision can only be made after considering information on both costs and benefits.

APPENDIX: CRS SENSITIVITY ANALYSIS

In an effort to assess the sensitivity of Crain and Crain's results, CRS ran a linear regression using similar, but somewhat different, data and methods.[104] Specifically, CRS compiled a dataset for 30 OECD countries over the period 2002-2008 using the same dependent variable (GDP per capita in constant 2000 dollars) and four of the five independent variables that were used by Crain and Crain. The four identical independent variables were (1) the World Governance Indicators regulatory quality index, (2) broadband penetration rates, (3) country population, and (4) foreign trade as a percentage of GDP. Data for these four variables were obtained from the OECD website (http://www.oecd.org).

Crain and Crain also included one other variable in their analysis: primary school enrollment as a share of the eligible population. In their analysis, the associated coefficient had an unexpected negative sign (indicating that as primary school enrollment went up, GDP per capita went down). Crain and Crain told CRS that the negative coefficient could be due to "aging pyramid" demographic effects. In the CRS analysis, two variables were added to account for such demographic effects: the proportion of the population under 14 and the proportion of the population over 65. These variables were calculated from data obtained from the U.S. Census Bureau international population statistics.[105] These demographic measures may capture "aging pyramid" effects more directly than the primary education variable.

CRS ran a cross-country fixed effects panel estimator with year indicator variables. Natural logarithms of all variables except the regulatory quality index were used in the regression. Estimation results using Stata 11 xtreg procedure, using robust (White) standard errors that are used by most empirical researchers. Estimation results run with conventional standard errors, which are very similar, are available upon request.

The estimation output is shown in *Table A-1* below. The estimated coefficient on the World Governance Indicators regulatory quality index is very small and is not significantly different from zero. The coefficient on population is also statistically insignificant, although other estimated coefficients have expected signs and are statistically significant at conventional levels of confidence.

Table A-1. CRS Regression Analysis
Estimated determinants of log real GDP per capita

Independent Variables	Estimated Marginal Contribution	Robust Standard Error	t-statistic	P>|t|	95% Confidence Interval	
Regulatory Quality Index	0001609	.0217325 0.01		0.994	-.0442871	.0446089
Population (log)	.2132556	.2595086 0.82		0.418	-.317499	.7440102
Broadband Penetration Rate (log)	.0233723	.0035276 6.63		0.000	.0161575	.0305872
Percent Population Under 14 (log)	-1.449251	.1967557 -7.37		0.000	-1.851661	-1.04684
Percent Population Over 65 (log)	-.3208979	.1686001 -1.90		0.067	-.6657239	.0239281
Foreign Trade as % of GDP (log)	.1051034	.0493794 2.13		0.042	.0041111	.2060957
sigma_u	.6039017	sigma_e .0206743				
Rho	.99882937	(fraction of variance due to u_i)				

Source: CRS.

Notes: Estimated using fixed-effects ordinary least squares regression with year dummies. Huber/White robust standard errors are reported.

Number of observations = 210. Number of groups = 30. Observations per group: 7. F(12,29) = 86.57. R-square: within = 0.9003; between = 0.0521; overall = 0.0409. Corr(u_i, Xb) = -0.7610.

The point estimate of the coefficient regulatory quality index (.0001609) can be used to estimate the economic effect of shifting the United States from the 2008 regulatory quality index value (1.508) to the 2008 level of Ireland (1.856). According to that calculation which presumes that the regression specification reflects the true structure of the economy, that shift would result in an increase of $2.14 in per capita GDP (measured in year 2000 dollars). Because the point estimate of the effect of the regulatory quality index is so imprecise, however, the calculated effect of a hypothetical shift of U.S. regulatory quality to the Irish level is also imprecise.

One test statistic (rho, a measure of intercountry correlation) indicates that 99.9% of the variance in the model results from differences among countries, rather than time-series variation within countries. This could suggest that estimating the effects of variables that generally change slowly over time, such as the regulatory environment in economically advanced countries, may be challenging using panel estimation methods the employ highly aggregated country-level data. Other econometric approaches that focus on more specific changes in regulatory environment may provide a better path for understanding the effects of regulation on economic activity.

End Notes

[1] The current requirement is in Section 624 of the Treasury and General Government Appropriations Act, 2001, (31 U.S.C. § 1105 note), sometimes referred to as the "Regulatory Right-to-Know Act."

[2] See http://www.sba.gov/sites/default/files/rs371tot.pdf to view a copy of this report. Hereafter, this report is referred to as "Crain and Crain." In addition to estimating the annual cost of federal regulations, the report also provided information indicating that regulatory costs fall particularly hard on small businesses. The report was developed under a contract with the SBA Office of Advocacy (contract number SBAHQ-08-M0466). Although the report cover states that it "contains information and analysis that was reviewed and edited by officials of the Office of Advocacy," it also says that the "final conclusions of the report do not necessarily reflect the views of the Office of Advocacy."

[3] Thomas D. Hopkins, "Profiles in Regulatory Costs," available at http://www.sba.gov/ sites/ default /files/files/rs1995hoptot.pdf.

[4] W. Mark Crain and Thomas D. Hopkins, "The Impact of Regulatory Costs on Small Firms," available at http://www.sba.gov/sites/default/files/files/rs207tot.pdf. For an analysis of this estimate, see CRS Report RL32339, *Federal Regulations: Efforts to Estimate Total Costs and Benefits of Rules*, by Curtis W. Copeland.

[5] W. Mark Crain, "The Impact of Regulatory Costs on Small Firms," available at http://www. sba.gov/sites/default/files/files/rs264tot.pdf.

[6] See, for example, Chad Moutrey, "To cure the economy, fix the business environment," *Washington Post*, January 10, 2011, available at http://www.washingtonpost.com/wp-dyn/content/article/2011/01/07/AR2011010705681.html;__"Obama's reformer disguise; Accountability is the solution to government red tape," *Washington Times*, January 26, 2011, p. B2; and Mark Tapscott, "Washington is the Reason the Economy Is Not Growing," *The Examiner*, December 2, 2010, p. 39.

[7] See, for example, testimony of Thomas M. Sullivan, before the House Committee on Education and Workforce, Subcommittee on Workforce Protections, February 15, 2011, available at http://edworkforce.house.gov/UploadedFiles/02.15.11_sullivan.pdf; and testimony of Karen Harned, before the House Committee on the Judiciary, Subcommittee on Courts, Commercial and Administrative Law, February 10, 2011, available at http://judiciary. house.gov/hearings/ pdf/Harned02102011.pdf.

[8] See, for example, Senator Dan Coats, "Coats Says Excessive Regulation is Hindering Private Sector Job Growth," Press Statement in support of S. 358, February 16, 2011, available at http://coats.senate.gov/newsroom/press/release/? id=F6E06668-FE12-460E-9D04-4ED6 11

EAB111; Opening statement of Representative Sam Graves, Chairman, House Committee on Small Business, February 16, 2011, available at http://smbiz.house.gov/UploadedFiles/2011.02.16_State_of_SmBiz_Opening.pdf; and a letter to President Barack Obama by four House committee chairmen, available at http://geoffdavis.house.gov/ UploadedFiles/POTUS_Letter_031011.pdf.

9 See, for example, http://www.geoffdavis.house.gov/Legislation/reins.htm, and http://www.geoffdavis.house.gov/ News/DocumentSingle.aspx?DocumentID=208463, in support of the "Regulations from the Executive In Need of Scrutiny (REINS) Act," H.R. 10 in the 112th Congress; http://snowe.senate.gov/public/index.cfm/pressreleases? Content Record_id=49fe01bb-b475-4ff1-b9e1-ea6eda50b7e&ContentType_id=ae7a6475-a01f-4da5-aa94-0a98973de620&Group_id=2643ccf9-0d03-4d09-9082-3807031cb84a &Month Display=3&YearDisplay=2011, in support of the Small Business Regulatory Freedom Act of 2011, S. 474 in the 112th Congress; and H.Rept. 112-6, "Directing Certain Standing Committees to Inventory and Review Existing, Pending, and Proposed Regulations and Orders from Agencies of the Federal Government, Particularly With Respect to Their Effect on Jobs and Economic Growth," Report to accompany H.Res. 72, February 8, 2011.

10 Carl Bialik, "The Numbers Guy: Small Business Regulatory 'Burden' Is Tough to Quantify," *Wall Street Journal*, January 29, 2011, p. A2; and Sidney A. Shapiro, Ruth Ruttenberg, and James Goodwin, "Setting the Record Straight: The Crain and Crain Report on Regulatory Costs," Center for Progressive Reform White Paper #1103, February 2011, available at http://www.progressivereform.org/articles/SBA_Regulatory_Costs_Analysis_1103.pdf ("CPR report").

11 Crain and Crain, p. 17.

12 Ibid.

13 In addition to "regulatory quality," the WGI indices include five other governance indicators: "voice and accountability," "political stability and absence of violence," "government effectiveness," "rule of law," and "control of corruption." The WGI methodology is described in Kaufmann, Kraay and Mastruzzi (2010). "The Worldwide Governance Indicators: Methodology and Analytical Issues" World Bank Policy Research Working Paper No. 5430, http://papers.ssrn.com/sol3/papers.cfm?abstract_id=1682130.

14 Crain and Crain, p. 19.

15 Ibid., p. 24.

16 Regression analysis is used to understand how the value of a dependent variable (e.g., real GDP per capita) changes when one of the independent variables is varied (e.g., the index of regulatory quality), while the other independent variables (e.g., country population) are held fixed.

17 Here, and elsewhere in the Crain and Crain report, cost estimates are provided for 2008 in 2009 dollars. It is unclear why Crain and Crain used 2009 dollars to present cost estimates for 2008.

18 See http://info.worldbank.org/governance/wgi/pdf/rq.pdf. Documentation for each individual source is available at http://info.worldbank.org/governance/wgi/sources.htm.

19 See, for example, M.A. Thomas, "What Do the Worldwide Governance Indicators Measure? *European Journal of Development Research*, vol. 22 (2010), pp. 31-54.

20 Daniel Kauffman, Aart Kraay, and Massimo Mastruzzi, "Response to 'What Do the Worldwide Governance Indicators Measure?'" *European Journal of Development Research*, vol. 22 (2010), pp. 55-58.

21 Daniel Kaufman, Aart Kraay, and Massimo Mastruzzi, "Governance Matters VIII: Aggregate and Individual Governance Indicators 1996 – 2008," World Bank Development Research

Group, Macroeconomics and Growth Team, Policy Research Working Paper 4978, June 2009.

[22] See G. Nicoletti, Scarpetta, and O. Boylaud, "Summary Indicators of Product Market Regulation and Employment Protection Legislation for the Purpose of International Comparisons," OECD Economics Department Working Paper No. 226 (2000).

[23] World Bank, "World Governance Indicators: Frequently Asked Questions," available at http://info.worldbank.org/ governance/wgi/faq.htm.

[24] Kraay provided CRS with a copy of his January 27, 2011, e-mail to Crain and Crain on March 4, 2011.

[25] In his comments to Crain and Crain, Kraay continued by saying that "one should not make a big deal of the fact that Sweden and Finland come in a bit ahead of the US, as the difference is not statistically significant (the margins of error overlap). But this does give you a good indication that WGI-RQ is not just measuring 'less regulation' as you seem to interpret it."

[26] Crain and Crain, p. 24.

[27] Carl Bialik, "The Numbers Guy: Small Business Regulatory 'Burden' Is Tough to Quantify," *Wall Street Journal*, January 29, 2011, p. A2.

[28] E-mail from Aart Kraay to Crain and Crain, January 27, 2011.

[29] E-mail to the author from Aart Kraay, World Bank, March 4, 2011.

[30] To view the data, see http://www-wds.worldbank.org/external/default/ WDSContentServer /IW3P /IB/2009/06/29/000158349_20090629095443/Rendered/PDF/WPS4978.pdf. Two other jurisdictions had higher scores than Ireland in 2008, but they are technically not countries (Hong Kong, at 1.998, and Singapore, at 1.918).

[31] E-mail to the author from Aart Kraay, World Bank, March 4, 2011.

[32] E-mail to the author from Nicole V. Crain and W. Mark Crain, March 7, 2011.

[33] The Ewing Marion Kauffman Foundation is described on its website as one of the largest foundations devoted to entrepreneurship. See http://www.kauffman.org/.

[34] The Mercatus Center is described on its website as the world's premier university source for market-oriented ideas. See http://mercatus.org/.

[35] According to a March 7, 2011, e-mail to the author from Radwan Saade of SBA's Office of Advocacy, the study was sent to the two peer reviewers "that identified as credible researchers and contributors to the discussion on regulatory costs." He said other researchers were contacted but were unavailable to serve as peer reviewers.

[36] Comments of Richard Williams, Mercatus Center, George Mason University, available at http://www.sba.gov/sites/default/files/files/TheImpactofFederalRegulatoryCostsonSmallFirmsPRFY2010.pdf.

[37] Williams said "You can start with the fundamental idea of opportunity costs. Resources that are devoted to complying with regulations are not used to produce GDP that responds to normal market forces (demand). Both activities, complying with regulations and normal market activities add to GDP. What has been estimated here is the difference between the two, GDP with resources that would have been devoted to normal market forces minus GDP with resources devoted to complying with regulation. That difference is, I think, one component of the cost of regulation. However, that may leave, (if I am thinking about this correctly) the cost of complying with regulation that is picked up by GDP. That is, a person can produce 10 widgets that comply with regulation and 15 widgets if employed normally by the market, and this model would estimate the costs of the regulation at 5 widgets (the difference in GDP). But that doesn't count the original 10 widgets of expenditure that adds to GDP and is also a cost and must be weighed against the benefits."

[38] Sidney A. Shapiro, Ruth Ruttenberg, and James Goodwin, "Setting the Record Straight: The Crain and Crain Report on Regulatory Costs," February 2011, available at http://www.progressivereform.org/articles/SBA_Regulatory_Costs_Analysis_1103.pdf. See http://www.progressivereform.org/articles/SBA_Letter_020811.pdf for a copy of the letter requesting that SBA's Office of Advocacy withdraw its sponsorship of the Crain and Crain report. In a March 11, 2011, letter to CPR, the Chief Counsel of SBA's Office of Advocacy said that he disagreed with CPR's assessment, and stood behind the findings of the Crain and Crain report.

[39] Ibid., pp. 4-6.

[40] This section of the report was written by D. Andrew Austin, Analyst in Economic Policy, Congressional Research Service.

[41] The OECD has 34 member states. Chile, Slovenia, and Israel joined in 2010, and Estonia is in the final stages of formal accession. Some historical data for those new entrants is unavailable. See OECD website (http://www.oecd.org) for details.

[42] Rudiger Dornbusch, Stanley Fischer, and Richard Startz, *Macroeconomics* (10th ed.), (New York: McGraw-Hill, 2008), ch. 1 and 2.

[43] Randall G. Holcombe, *Public Finance*, (Minneapolis: West, 1996).

[44] For details on the linear regression model and its statistical properties, see Peter Kennedy, *A Guide to Econometrics* (4th Edition), (Cambridge, Massachusetts: MIT Press, 1998), ch. 3, "The Classical Linear Regression Model."

[45] In another study, Crain and Crain used a measure of equipment investment in an article that example determinants of GDP per capita for a sample of 99 countries. See Nicole V. Crain and W. Mark Crain, "Terrorized Economies," *Public Choice*, vol. 128, pp.317-349.

[46] Badi Baltagi, *Econometric Analysis of Panel Data* (4th ed.), (New York: Wiley, 2008). If certain technical conditions hold, this approach can generate estimates with desirable statistical properties. See William H. Greene, *Econometric Analysis* (New York: Prentice Hall, 2003), ch. 13, "Models for Panel Data."

[47] See notes to Table 2 in Crain and Crain (2010).

[48] The primary education variable was replaced with two demographic variables: the proportion of the population under age 14, and the proportion of the population over age 65. The data were for 30 OECD countries for the same time period as the Crain and Crain study (2002 – 2008). The analysis used a standard fixed-effects panel estimator with year dummy variables.

[49] See http://www.whitehouse.gov/sites/default/files/omb/assets/omb/inforeg/ costbenefitreport.pdf for OMB's 2001 report.

[50] Robert W. Hahn and John A. Hird, "The Costs and Benefits of Regulation: Review and Synthesis," *Yale Journal of Regulation,* vol. 8 (1991), pp. 233-278. Hahn and Hird provided estimates for all rules issued prior to 1988. The estimate for rules issued from 1987 through the first quarter of 2000 were from agencies' estimates of all rules.

[51] In its 2001 report, OMB estimated environmental costs as of the first quarter of 2000 at between $96 billion and $170 billion, in 1996 dollars. In 2001 dollars, Crain and Crain said the costs were between $108.359 billion and $191.887 billion.

[52] See http://www.whitehouse.gov/sites/default/files/omb /assets/omb/inforeg/2002_ report_to_ congress.pdf for OMB's 2002 report. In this and all subsequent reports, OMB's estimates were in 2001 dollars. As used in this report, the term "major rule" includes all rules meeting the definition in the Congressional Review Act (5 U.S.C. § 804(2) (e.g., an annual effect on the economy of $100 million or more). For a discussion of "major rules," see CRS Report

R41651, *REINS Act: Number and Types of "Major Rules" in Recent Years*, by Curtis W. Copeland and Maeve P. Carey.

[53] Crain and Crain, p. 27. In a March 7, 2011, e-mail to the author, Crain and Crain noted that the OMB data do not include regulations whose costs are expected to be below $100 million, or costs that are not monetized. Therefore, they said, using the upper bound is an attempt to correct for this omission in a systemic and reasonable way. They also said that agency cost estimates are unlikely to include costs associated with negotiated enforcement.

[54] See http://www.whitehouse.gov/sites/default/files/omb/assets/omb/inforeg/2000fedreg-report.pdf, p. 15.

[55] See http://www.whitehouse.gov/sites/default/files/omb/assets/omb/inforeg/2004_cb_final.pdf, p. 7, Table 1.

[56] See http://www.whitehouse.gov/sites/default/files/omb/assets/omb/inforeg/ 2005_cb/final_2005_cb_report.pdf, Table 1-3. The $3,840 million to $4,073 million cost estimate in this report is for rules issued by the Departments of Health and Human Services and Transportation, and the Environmental Protection Agency.

[57] E-mail to the author from Nicole V. Crain and W. Mark Crain, March 7, 2011.

[58] Crain and Crain, p. 25.

[59] Crain and Crain, p. 27.

[60] Ibid.

[61] Ibid, footnote 27. Actually, the Harrington study concluded that agencies' estimates of direct costs appeared to be too high in 12 rules, and too low in 6 rules. The authors' conclusions regarding per-unit abatement costs only applied to EPA and OSHA regulations. See Winston Harrington, et al., "On the Accuracy of Regulatory Cost Estimates," available at http://www.rff.org/documents/RFF-DP-99-18.pdf.

[62] Sidney A. Shapiro, Ruth Ruttenberg, and James Goodwin, "Setting the Record Straight: The Crain and Crain Report on Regulatory Costs," p. 7.

[63] Office of Management and Budget, "Appendix: Summary of Public Comments," available at http://www.whitehouse.gov/omb/inforeg_appendix.

[64] The Tax Foundation is a nonpartisan tax research group based in Washington, D.C. For more information, see http://www.taxfoundation.org/about/. Crain and Crain said they used information from the Tax Foundation's 2005 report, but did not provide a citation for that report.

[65] Office of Management and Budget, *Information Collection Budget: 2009* (reporting on FY2008), available at http://www.whitehouse.gov/sites/default/files/omb/assets /inforeg /icb _2009.pdf.

[66] See CRS Report R40636, *Paperwork Reduction Act (PRA): OMB and Agency Responsibilities and Burden Estimates*, by Curtis W. Copeland and Vanessa K. Burrows.

[67] See http://www.bls.gov/oes/current/oes132082.htm for these data.

[68] For example, BLS data indicated that accountants and auditors were paid an average of $32.42 per hour in May 2009. See http://www.bls.gov/oes/current/oes132011.htm.

[69] Office of Management and Budget, *Report to Congress on the Costs and Benefits of Federal Regulations*, September 30, 1997, available at http://www.whitehouse.gov /omb /inforeg_rcongress/.

[70] See http://www.whitehouse.gov/omb/legislative_testimony_graham_030722_graham/ for a copy of this testimony.

[71] Cited by Crain and Crain as Joseph M. Johnson, "A Review and Synthesis of the Cost of Workplace Regulations, in *Cross-Border Human Resources*, Labor International: Netherlands, 2005, pp. 433-467.

[72] Although Crain and Crain said (in Table 5 on p. 30 of their report) that they only used rules issued between 2001 and 2008, the 2009 OMB report does not identify when the four Occupational Safety and Health Administration rules were issued. Also, conversion of OMB's upper-end estimate for all four rules ($389 million in 2001 dollars) into 2009 dollars yields an estimate of $471 million—the same figure used in Crain and Crain's report.

[73] Crain and Crain, p. 27. In a March 7, 2011, e-mail to the author, Crain and Crain noted that the OMB data do not include regulations whose costs are expected to be below $100 million, or costs that are not monetized. Therefore, they said, using the upper bound is an attempt to correct for this omission in a systemic and reasonable way. They also said that agency cost estimates are unlikely to include costs associated with negotiated enforcement.

[74] Office of Management and Budget, "Appendix: Summary of Public Comments," available at http://www.whitehouse.gov/omb/inforeg_appendix.

[75] CPR, p. 9.

[76] Crain and Crain said that the $1.1 trillion estimate of regulatory costs in 2004 would be $1.26 trillion in 2009 dollars.

[77] Crain and Crain, p. 20. The authors said that the 2005 study used an index of economic regulations developed by the Organization for Economic Cooperation and Development (OECD), supplemented by information from the International Trade Commission and other sources. Crain and Crain said they used the World Bank index of regulatory quality because it was a more comprehensive index of economic regulations. Had the 2005 study used the methodology used in the 2010 study, the authors said that the total cost would have been $1.7 trillion, an increase of $43 billion between 2004 and 2008 after adjusting for inflation.

[78] See http://www.whitehouse.gov/omb/inforeg_rcongress/ for a copy of this report.

[79] See http://www.whitehouse.gov/sites/default/files/omb/assets/omb/inforeg/costbenefitreport 1998.pdf, Table 3.

[80] See http://www.whitehouse.gov/sites/default/files/omb/assets/omb/inforeg/costbenefitreport. pdf, Table 2.

[81] See http://www.whitehouse.gov/omb/inforeg_chap2.

[82] See http://www.whitehouse.gov/sites/default/files/omb/assets/omb/inforeg/costbenefitreport 1998.pdf, p. 1.

[83] Specifically, in its 1997 report, OMB said "studies that have attempted to tote up the total costs and benefits of Federal regulations have basically added together a diverse set of individual studies. Unfortunately, these individual studies vary in quality, methodology, and type of regulatory costs included. Thus we have an apples and oranges problem, or, more aptly, an apples, oranges, kiwis, grapefruit, etc., problem." See http://www.whitehouse. gov/ omb/ inforeg_chap2.

[84] Office of Management and Budget, Office of Information and Regulatory Affairs, Stimulating Smarter Regulation: 2002 Report to Congress on the Costs and Benefits of Regulations and Unfunded Mandates on State, Local, and Tribal Entities, 2002, available at http://www. whitehouse.gov/sites/default/files/omb/assets/omb/inforeg/2002_report_to_ congress.pdf.

[85] Office of Management and Budget, Office of Information and Regulatory Affairs, Informing Regulatory Decisions: 2003 Report to Congress on the Costs and Benefits of Federal Regulations and Unfunded Mandates on State, Local, and Tribal Entities, 2003, available at http://www.whitehouse.gov/sites/default/files/omb/assets/omb/inforeg/2003_cost-ben_ final_ rpt.pdf.

[86] See http://www.whitehouse.gov/sites/default/files/omb/assets/omb/inforeg/2002_ report_ to_ congress.pdf, p. 40.

[87] Ibid., p. 41. Section 515 of the Treasury and General Government Appropriations Act for Fiscal Year 2001, generally known as the "Data Quality Act" or the "Information Quality Act," amended the Paperwork Reduction Act and directed OMB to issue government-wide guidelines that "provide policy and procedural guidance to Federal agencies for ensuring and maximizing the quality, objectivity, utility, and integrity of information (including statistical information) disseminated by Federal agencies."

[88] See http://www.whitehouse.gov/sites/default/files/omb/assets/omb/inforeg/2003_cost-ben_final_rpt.pdf, p. 7. In its 2010 report to Congress, OMB continues to say that estimates that are more than 10 years old are of "questionable relevance." See http://www. whitehouse. gov/sites/default/files/omb/legislative/reports/2010_Benefit_ Cost_ Report.pdf, p. 11.

[89] Testimony of John D. Graham before the House Committee on Government Reform, July 22, 2003, available at http://www.whitehouse.gov/omb/legislative_ testimony_graham_ 030722 _graham.

[90] "Chief of OMB Regulatory Review Opposes Ose Bill on Regulatory Accounting, Budgeting," *BNA Daily Report for Executives*, July 23, 2003, p. A-43.

[91] OMB's 2009 report to Congress, p. 9.

[92] Ibid.

[93] Ibid., p. 8.

[94] OMB's report did, however, provide some information on rules issued by certain independent regulatory agencies (e.g., the Board of Governors of the Federal Reserve System and the Securities and Exchange Commission) as provided to OMB by the Government Accountability Office. The agencies typically did not provide information on costs and benefits.

[95] Office of Management and Budget, *Report to Congress on the Costs and Benefits of Federal Regulations*, September 30, 1997, available at http://www.whitehouse.gov/omb/ inforeg_ rcongress/.

[96] Ibid.

[97] Crain and Crain, p. 10.

[98] E-mail to the author from Nicole V. Crain and W. Mark Crain, March 7, 2011.

[99] E-mail to the author from Radwan Saade, SBA Office of Advocacy, March 7, 2011. See https://www.fbo.gov/?s= opportunity&mode=form&tab=core&id=8ffd890376c03038eb0e7f3fa657f7c1&_cview=1 to view the solicitation for this study.

[100] Executive Order 12866, "Regulatory Planning and Review," 58 *Federal Register* 51735, Oct. 4, 1993.

[101] See http://www.whitehouse.gov/sites/default/files/omb/legislative/reports/2010_Benefit_ Cost_Report.pdf for a copy of this report.

[102] See http://www.whitehouse.gov/sites/default/files/omb/legislative/reports/ Draft_2011_ CBA_ Report_AllSections.pdf for a copy of this report.

[103] E-mail to the author from Nicole V. Crain and W. Mark Crain, March 7, 2011.

[104] This appendix was written by D. Andrew Austin, Analyst in Economic Policy, Congressional Research Service.

[105] The U.S. Census Bureau International Population Data Base is available at http://www.census. gov/ipc/www/idb/informationGateway.php. The regulatory quality index was taken from the World Bank's World Governance Indicators website, available at http://info.worldbank. org/governance/wgi/index.asp. The OECD data were taken from data portal available at http://www.oecd.org.

In: Federal Regulatory Costs ISBN: 978-1-61470-389-1
Editors: R. N. Marapao, C. G. Abulog

Chapter 2

The Impact of Regulatory Costs on Small Firms*

Nicole V. Crain and W. Mark Crain

Executive Summary

The annual cost of federal regulations in the United States increased to more than $1.75 trillion in 2008. Had every U.S. household paid an equal share of the federal regulatory burden, each would have owed $15,586 in 2008. By comparison, the federal regulatory burden exceeds by 50 percent private spending on health care, which equaled $10,500 per household in 2008. While all citizens and businesses pay some portion of these costs, the distribution of the burden of regulations is quite uneven. The portion of regulatory costs that falls initially on businesses was $8,086 per employee in 2008. Small businesses, defined as firms employing fewer than 20 employees, bear the largest burden of federal regulations. As of 2008, small businesses face an annual regulatory cost of $10,585 per employee, which is 36 percent higher than the regulatory cost facing large firms (defined as firms with 500 or more employees).

The regulatory landscape highlighted above and detailed in this report emerges from an updated analysis of the regulatory record explored in three

* This is an edited, reformatted and augmented version of a SBA Office of Advocacy publication, dated September, 2010.

previous studies for the Office of the Chief Counsel for Advocacy of the U.S. Small Business Administration (Hopkins, 1995; Crain and Hopkins, 2001; and Crain, 2005). Direct comparisons to the results in these prior studies should be made with caution, however. The present study introduces some new methodological techniques, which may account for some of the differences in the cost estimates for 2008 versus those for prior years.

I. PURPOSE AND HIGHLIGHTS

Government regulations pervade modern life in America and other nations with few exceptions. Regulations are needed to provide the rules and structure for societies to properly function. This research, while mindful of this fact, does not consider the benefits of federal regulations, but looks at the overall costs imposed by them. Little stock is taken of the cumulative effects.

Unlike most fiscal actions taken by government, the costs of regulatory actions are relatively hidden. For example, consider the activities, products, and services consumed by a typical household on a typical day. The costs of government regulations get stirred into the indistinct mixture of countless economic forces that determine prices, costs, designs, locations, profits, losses, wages, dividends, and so forth. Isolating the contribution of regulations to one's daily routine requires more than simply looking at the sales receipts, for example, as in the case of government sales taxes. A comprehensive list of regulatory influences that affect one's daily existence is indeed extensive and overwhelming to track or sum up. Yet, knowledge of the cumulative consequences of regulatory actions, and how these are changing, provides important information to assess and evaluate the performance of a political-economic social system.

This report seeks to fill some of these gaps in our knowledge by providing estimates of the costs of federal government regulations in the United States. An awareness of regulatory costs reveals much about the balance in public versus private sector responsibilities for and control over resources. Transparency about compliance costs can inform critical judgments about what society gives up in exchange for government responsibility exercised through the machinery of the regulatory process.

Policymakers long ago recognized the importance of information about U.S. taxing and spending programs; such fiscal information has been provided systematically for nearly a century and is in fact mandated by the Constitution (Article 1, Section 9). The annual federal budget process and the *Budget of the*

United States provide considerable detail regarding where the money comes from and how it is spent. The quest for transparency in the nation's fiscal affairs has increased through the online availability of and public access to detailed budget information.

Unfortunately, comparable information about the impact of federal regulatory programs is largely absent. Federal regulations escaped any rigorous scrutiny until limited tracking was mandated by Executive Order 11821 in 1974. The federal Regulatory Right-to-Know Act, enacted in 2000, was a major attempt to make information about the costs and benefits of regulations far more transparent and widely available than before. This act requires the U.S. Office of Management and Budget (OMB) to submit an accounting statement and report that includes an estimate of the total annual costs and benefits of federal rules and paperwork "to the extent feasible."[1]

In the 2009 Report from OMB, the estimated annual cost of major federal regulations ranges between $51 billion and $60 billion in 2001 dollars. Denominated in 2009 dollars (that is, adjusting for inflation), this annual cost is between $62 billion and $73 billion. The estimated cost range provided in OMB's report differs markedly from estimates in three prior studies commissioned by the Office of Advocacy of the U.S. Small Business Administration (hereafter referred to as "Advocacy").[2] Thomas Hopkins (1995) estimated annual federal regulatory costs to be $777 billion. Mark Crain and Thomas Hopkins (2001) estimated the annual costs to be $876 billion (both numbers are converted here to 2001 dollars, the base year normally used by OMB in its reports). More recently, Crain (2005) estimated the annual costs to be in excess of $1 trillion (again in 2001 dollars). According to these three studies for Advocacy, the costs of federal regulations are larger than the costs reported by OMB by a factor of 13 to 17. What accounts for this large discrepancy?

OMB discusses this issue openly and candidly, stating in its 2009 *Report*: "because these estimates exclude non major rules and rules adopted more than ten years ago, the total benefits and costs of all Federal rules now in effect are likely to be significantly larger than the sum of the benefits and costs reported."[3]

It is worth emphasizing at the beginning of this report the main factors that cause OMB's estimates to differ so greatly from those in the studies for Advocacy, including the new estimates presented here for 2008. If OMB or other government-provided estimates were complete and comprehensive, further study would add little value. First, in compiling its accounting statement, OMB includes only those regulations that it cleared during the previous 10 years, which in the 2009 report included October 1, 1998, to September 30, 2008. Limiting the analysis to this time period omits some of the most costly federal regulations, such as the regulations stemming from the parts of the Clean Air Act and its amendments that were enacted before 1998.

Second, the annual OMB accounting statements are based solely on cost-benefit analyses that were performed by the separate federal agencies.[4] In other words, the sources for the cost and benefit estimates that OMB uses to compile its accounting statement are the federal agencies that promulgate and enforce regulations, and those agencies frequently declare many costs to be "inestimable." This means that while the annual OMB accounting statements offer a trove of relevant information, the coverage in these annual statements is limited; federal agencies have not assessed the costs (or the benefits) for a host of regulatory activities — past and present. This is particularly problematic in the case of economic regulations, which have not been analyzed by federal agencies and therefore have not been included in OMB's annual accounting total. Burdensome economic regulations such as import restrictions, antitrust policies, telecommunications policies, product safety laws, and many other restraints on business activities are implemented outside of the OMB regulatory review process.[5] None of these regulatory costs are therefore included in OMB's annual estimates of total costs.

Third, the OMB annual reports to Congress include "major" regulations reviewed by OMB. This methodological decision is understandable given the massive volume of "non major" regulations. Nonetheless, thousands of non major regulations in the aggregate may amount to substantial costs. Fourth, and finally, a host of regulations are issued by independent regulatory agencies — federal government entities that fall outside the executive branch — and, therefore, are not subject to the reporting requirements in Executive Order 12866.[6] The costs and benefits of such regulations are not included in the aggregate costs and benefits reported by OMB.[7]

These and other differences between OMB's cost calculations and those used in this study will be described in further detail in the sections that follow. This preliminary discussion anticipates the natural question about the large difference between OMB's cost estimates and the cost estimates in Hopkins (1995), Crain and Hopkins (2001), Crain (2005), and those presented in this study. An appreciation of the limitations of OMB's regulatory accounting procedures also motivates one of the purposes of this study, which is an inclusive accounting of all federal regulations and their estimated cost. The cost estimates provided by OMB — in general, calculated by the specific executive branch agency that promulgated the regulation — are used whenever possible in this report, in particular for environmental regulations, occupational safety and health, and homeland security regulations. In the case of regulatory activities for which OMB does not offer cost estimates, the report performs independent analysis to approximate the costs and relies on other secondary sources. For example, the report specifies and estimates an econometric model and then uses the parameters to estimate the cost of economic regulations.

This report seeks to update and improve the 1995, 2001, and 2005 studies for Advocacy and advance the understanding of who bears what burdens from regulation. In particular, the report seeks to identify the federal regulatory burden on small U.S. firms, and to assess whether and to what extent this burden disadvantages small businesses relative to their larger competitors. Underlying the significance of this assessment for the U.S. economy is the fact that 89 percent of all firms in the United States employ fewer than 20 workers. By comparison, large firms (defined as those with 500 or more employees) account for only 0.3 percent of all U.S. firms.[8] If federal regulations place a differentially large cost on small business, this potentially causes inefficiencies in the structure of American enterprises, and the relocation of production facilities to less regulated countries, and adversely affects the international competitiveness of domestically produced American products and services. All of these effects, of course, would have negative consequences for the U.S. labor market and national income.

Some Key Findings: The Cost of Federal Regulations in 2008

The findings in this report indicate that in 2008, U.S. federal government regulations cost an estimated $1.75 trillion, an amount equal to 14 percent of U.S. national income. When combined with U.S. federal tax receipts, which equaled 21 percent of national income in 2008, these two costs of federal government programs in 2008 consumed 35 percent of national income. This obviously represents a substantial burden on U.S. citizens and businesses.

It is important to stress that direct comparisons between 2008 and prior years must be made cautiously because new estimation methodologies introduced in this study were not possible previously. This means that some of the cost differences are attributable to different estimation techniques. Given this cautionary caveat, the comparable cost in 2004 was an estimated $1.26 trillion (in 2009 dollars), or 11 percent of national income (Crain, 2005).[9] If regulatory costs in 2004 are recomputed using the methodologies introduced in this study, those costs rise by $445 billion to an estimated $1.7 trillion (again, converted into 2009 dollars). This apples-to-apples comparison — that is, using the same estimation methods —suggests that the cost of federal regulations increased by $43 billion (or three percent) between 2004 and 2008 after adjusting for inflation.

What is the distribution of federal regulatory costs among firms of different sizes? The findings in this report indicate that compliance costs fall disproportionately on small businesses. Table 1 summarizes the incidence of costs by firm size based on aggregate data for all sectors of the U.S. economy.

Considering all federal regulations, all sectors of the U.S. economy, and all firm sizes, federal regulations cost $8,086 per employee per year in 2008. For firms with fewer than 20 employees, the cost is $10,585 per employee per year.

Table 1. Distribution of Regulatory Compliance Costs by Firm Size in 2008 *

	Cost per Employee			
Type of Regulation	All Firms	Firms with <20 Employees	Firms with 20-499 Employees	Firms with 500+ Employees
All Federal Regulations	$8,086	$10,585	$7,454	$7,755
Economic	$5,153	$4,120	$4,750	$5,835
Environmental	$1,523	$4,101	$1,294	$883
Tax Compliance	$800	$1,584	$760	$517
Occupational Safety and Health, and Homeland Security	$610	$781	$650	$520

* Notes to Table 1: Costs are denominated in 2009 dollars. The cost per employee for each firm size category uses employment shares for the respective business sectors to compute the weighted averages.

The cost is $7,454 in medium-sized firms, and $7,755 in large firms. Costs per employee thus appear to be at least 36 percent higher in small firms than in medium-sized and large firms. These results are roughly consistent with the findings in Hopkins (1995), Crain and Hopkins (2001), Crain (2005), as well as other studies completed during the past 25 years.[10]

The underlying force driving this differential cost burden is easy to understand. Many of the costs associated with regulatory compliance are "fixed costs," that is, a firm with five employees incurs roughly the same expense as a firm with 500 employees. In large firms, these fixed costs of compliance are spread over a large revenue, output, and employee base, which results in lower costs per unit of output as firm size increases. This is the familiar empirical phenomenon known as economies of scale, and its impact is to provide a comparative cost advantage to large firms over small firms.

The findings in Table 1 illustrate that the compliance cost disadvantage faced by small businesses is driven by environmental regulations, tax compliance, occupational safety and health, and homeland security regulations. The cost per employee of environmental regulations is more than four times higher in small firms than in large firms. With respect to tax compliance, the cost per employee is three times higher in small firms than in large firms. The particular drivers of the distribution of compliance costs among firm sizes differ across sectors of the U.S. economy. Later sections of the report lay out these patterns in further detail. It is worth highlighting the finding that not all regulations fall more heavily on small businesses than on larger firms. For example, the cost per employee of economic regulations falls most heavily on large firms. In part, this likely reflects the fact some industrial structures do not lend themselves to small firm participation (*e.g.*, utilities, telecoms, or mining) because large scale operations are a precondition to remain competitive. This simply reduces the number of small enterprises that would be affected. Another factor impacting the distribution of economic regulations is the Regulatory Flexibility Act (RFA). Under the RFA agencies are required to assess the effect of regulations on small businesses, and to mitigate undue burdens, including exemptions and relaxed phase-in schedules.[11]

This report details the distribution of regulatory costs for five major sectors of the U.S. economy: manufacturing, trade (wholesale and retail), services, health care (including social assistance), and "other" (a residual category containing all businesses not included in the other four).[12] This is the same five-sector grouping that was used in the prior report for SBA. The sector-specific findings reveal that the disproportionate cost burden on small firms is most dramatic in the manufacturing sector; the compliance cost per employee for small manufacturers is more than double the compliance cost for medium-sized and large firms. In the health care sector and the "other" sector categories, the compliance costs also appear starkly higher in small firms compared with medium-sized and large firms. In the service and trade sectors, the distribution of regulatory costs among firm sizes is much more even overall, yet varies depending on the type of regulation.

The remainder of the report is organized into three sections and four appendices. Section II gives an overview of the regulatory accounting methodology and describes the primary sources for the cost estimates used in the report. Section III begins with a snapshot of American enterprise, showing the distribution of firms, employees, and payroll expenditures for the major sectors of the U.S. economy. It then presents the underlying assumptions and maps the methods used to allocate: (i) the regulatory burden that falls on business, (ii) the regulatory costs across business sectors, and (iii) the regulatory costs by firm size within each business sector. Section IV provides the detailed findings for the distribution of the costs across the sectors and firm sizes, and by type of regulation. The appendices contain details for the various analytical procedures used in the report, and supplemental information about the "on-budget" expenditures on federal regulatory agencies.

This report does not address the benefits of regulation, an important challenge that would be a logical next step toward achieving a rational regulatory system. The annual accounting statements compiled by OMB move toward such a system by presenting partial estimates of benefits as well as costs. This report, thus, should be seen as a building block toward a broader understanding of the costs of regulation, much of which creates important and substantial benefits. Like data on federal budgetary outcomes, the regulatory cost estimates inform the discussion about the balance between public and private sector control over resources.

II. Scope of Regulatory Costs

Perspective on Regulatory Accounting

The imbalance between what is known about the costs and benefits of government regulations versus government fiscal programs is hardly surprising. Regulatory accounting requires the discovery of relevant costs and benefits not reflected in any governmental cash flow, which is inherently a difficult task. Fiscal accounting is simpler in two respects: it has the luxury of using well documented monetary flows tied to tax receipts and agency expenditures, and it tracks costs but not the associated benefits. Notwithstanding the practical difficulties associated with regulatory accounting, the impact of government regulations on business and citizen activities is no less real than the impact of fiscal programs.

The total direct cost of federal regulations consists of resources employed by government agencies to promulgate, monitor, and enforce regulations, as well as the compliance activities by citizens and enterprises. This report follows the practice in the three predecessor studies for Advocacy by focusing on the latter: the resource costs over and above those that show up in the federal budget and agency personnel charts. The report provides an accounting of the nonbudgeted costs imposed on individuals and businesses to comply with regulations. A simple example illustrates this perspective on regulatory accounting. The total direct cost to the nation of, say, a pollution control regulation consists of spending by the U.S. Environmental Protection Agency for monitoring and enforcement activities, plus spending by businesses to install abatement equipment, hire environmental engineers, attorneys, accountants, and so on to comply with the regulatory rules. EPA spending shows up in the federal budget, and therefore would not be included in this report's cost accounting. Rather, this report includes estimates of the impact on those who are regulated: the spending by businesses to install abatement equipment, hire engineers, and so forth. In this sense, the estimates presented understate the full cost of federal regulations.

Regulatory agency spending — the cost component this report excludes — amounts to less than 3 percent of the nonbudgeted regulatory compliance costs on which this report focuses. Nonetheless, spending by federal regulatory agencies on regulatory activity reached $47 billion in fiscal year 2008, so it is not trivial. Appendix 4 provides the on-budget costs of federal regulations, and shows how these budgets have grown over time. Between 1990 and 2008 regulatory agency budgets grew by 129 percent in inflation-adjusted dollars, an average annual rate of about 7 percent.[13] Total staffing of federal regulatory activity in fiscal year 2008 equaled 249,471 full-time equivalent employees. These staffing levels grew by 63 percent between 1990 and 2008, or 4 percent on an annualized basis. While these on-budget indicators of federal regulatory costs are large and growing, they represent only a tiny fraction of the nonbudgeted compliance costs on which this report focuses. To reiterate, on-budget spending on federal regulatory activity equals only 2.7 percent of the estimated compliance costs borne by U.S. citizens and businesses.

Other important regulatory costs are not captured in this report's estimates, most notably activities by state and local governments, indirect burdens, and general equilibrium effects. Regulatory agencies in the 50 American states have promulgated hundreds of thousands of regulations that are superimposed on federal regulations. Consider state-level environmental regulations as just one example. The sections of the State Administrative Codes that regulate the environment consist of 18 million words.[14] The costs of complying with hundreds of thousands of state regulations are not explicitly considered here, but clearly add to the nation's total regulatory compliance burden.[15]

The report uses various methods to determine how the costs of regulations are distributed: between businesses and individuals, among sectors of the U.S. economy, and among businesses of different sizes. These tend to reflect the initial or statutory burden of the regulations, that is, based on who bears the initial compliance costs. It needs to be acknowledged that this initial compliance burden can be shifted, and the final incidence of regulations may differ from this initial or statutory assignment of the regulatory costs. The difference between the initial incidence and how costs are ultimately divided depends on the demand and supply elasticities in the respective product and input markets. The final incidence of the federal regulatory burden is likely to differ from the initial incidence of costs. Of course, this is exactly analogous to the distinction between how a government collects a tax versus who ultimately pays for the tax. Collecting 100 percent of gasoline taxes from the service station owner does not necessarily mean that the owner bears the full burden of the gas tax. Rather, the gas tax is passed on to consumers to the extent they are willing to pay a higher price at the pump. While acknowledging that shifting in the cost burdens will occur, this report does not attempt to model these changes because the estimates of the relevant supply and demand elasticities for different sectors of the U.S. economy are not sufficiently consistent or reliable. This methodological issue is addressed again in Section III.

Similarly, the report does not account for a number of indirect or second-order costs of regulations. For example, environmental regulations directly affect the cost of producing electricity, and these show up as a direct cost for electric utilities. The report's cost estimates include these types of direct costs. Yet increases in the cost of electricity have ripple effects throughout the American economy in the form of higher energy costs, thus indirectly raising costs in virtually every sector. Some of these costs will be shifted even further onto consumers in the form of higher prices (directly for energy consumption, and, indirectly, for the other products purchased that now cost more because of higher energy costs). For another example, regulations that raise costs on health care providers will be shifted forward, at least partially depending on market elasticities, in the form of higher rates businesses must pay for health insurance premiums and other health care-related outlays. In turn, businesses will attempt to shift the burden of these higher health care-related outlays by increasing consumer prices or requiring employees to pay a larger share of health care costs. Some attempt is made to examine the more general impact of economic regulations, yet the distribution of these costs among sectors necessarily relies on the initial incidence.

Other general equilibrium effects include a reduction in dynamic efficiency, such as slowing innovations that would lead to productivity gains and therefore general economic expansions over time.[16] Again, the study does not measure the dynamic effects; omission of the indirect and general equilibrium effects means that the estimates in the report probably understate the full burden of federal regulations.[17]

As a rule, the approach used in this report to approximate the costs of regulations follows the methods used by Hopkins (1995), OMB annual reports (2000 through 2009), Crain and Hopkins (2001), and Crain (2005). This consistency helps to make the results comparable over time. As in past studies, new estimation techniques are adopted when these offer obvious improvements in the reliability and quality of the cost estimates. The introduction of new methodologies obviously means that comparisons to regulatory costs in prior years must be qualified.

Major Categories of Federal Regulations: Sources and Methods

The report divides federal regulations into four categories: economic; environmental; tax compliance; and occupational safety and health, and homeland security.[18] A description of each category follows, along with an explanation of the primary sources and methods used to derive the compliance cost estimates.

1. Economic Regulations

Economic regulations include a wide range of restrictions and incentives that affect the way businesses operate — what products and services they produce, how and where they produce them, and how products and services are priced and marketed to consumers. Economic regulations affect both domestic and international business operations. For example, laws that impose quotas and tariffs on foreign imports limit competition from outside the United States, restrict production and employment, raise prices, and generally curtail U.S. economic activity.

One of the major differences between the cost estimates in this study and the estimates reported by OMB in its Annual Reports to Congress is that OMB does not include regulations issued by agencies not subject to Executive Order 12866 — the independent regulatory agencies.[19] In its 2009 report, OMB discusses and recognizes the potentially large impact of such regulatory activity (OMB, 2009, pp. 29-34). Nonetheless, OMB has not implemented estimates for a host of economic regulations, beyond those for which it has reviewed regulatory impact statements submitted by federal agencies during the past 10 years. As noted in the introduction to this report, OMB recognizes the potentially large costs associated with regulatory activities not included in its annual estimates of total regulatory costs.

A methodology was introduced in the prior report for Advocacy (Crain 2005) to expand the coverage by providing a method to assess the costs of broad-based economic regulations. Obviously, the goal is to incorporate into the analysis the impact of the widest possible range of economic regulations, including those that are promulgated by independent regulatory agencies. The method employs cross-country regression analysis to examine the impact of a broad index of economic regulations on the national economic output (GDP).[20] The 2005 study used an index of economic regulations developed by the Organization for Economic Cooperation and Development (OECD). The cost estimate derived from this approach was referred to as the "baseline" estimate in the 2005 study, simply because the regression procedure accounted for most of the costs of economic regulations. That baseline estimate was then supplemented in two ways: (i) by a separate estimate of the cost of international trade regulations using data from the International Trade Commission, and (ii) with estimates for specific domestic economic regulations that were either not covered by the OECD index, or were promulgated in years after that index was computed. In other words, several different approaches were used in the 2005 study to compile an inclusive measure of the cost of economic regulations.

This study again uses the comparative, cross-country regression approach, in this case adopting an alternative index of economic regulations that is more comprehensive than the OECD index. This new index of economic regulations, labeled the Regulatory Quality Index, is computed by researchers at the World Bank as part of its Worldwide Governance Indicators (WGI) research project. The WGI project has estimated various measures of governance and institutional quality, including the Regulatory Quality Index used in this report. These indices are available from 1996 through 2008.

The Regulatory Quality Index measures perceptions of the ability of governments to formulate and implement sound policies and regulations that permit and promote private sector development. For example, the index values for 2008 are derived from 1,751 data points, representing four types of data: commercial business information providers (46 percent); public sector organizations (24 percent); nongovernmental organizations (17 percent); and surveys of firms or households (13 percent). The data from these four sources are aggregated using a statistical procedure known as the unobserved components model.[21] The elements included in the Regulatory Quality Index are listed in Appendix 1.

Three important aspects of the WGI Regulatory Quality Index — how it differs from the OECD economic regulation index used in Crain (2005) and why it enhances the accuracy of the estimated costs of economic regulation — should be described. First, a larger data series is available for the Regulatory Quality Index, covering a longer time period and more countries, and this helps to overcome the small sample size used to estimate the parameters in the Crain (2005) study.[22] Second, the Regulatory Quality Index covers international as well as domestic economic regulations. This means that unlike the 2005 study, a separate estimate of the international economic regulation component is unnecessary. Third, the WGI Regulatory Quality Index includes rules and mandates that affect factors markets — which obviously include the labor market — as well as product markets. This means that the impact of economic regulations that affect the workplace is encompassed in this measure. For this reason the four categories of regulations are redefined from the 2005 study. In that report, "workplace regulations" were a separate category and estimated using a different methodology. In this report, the estimated costs of workplace regulations, such as laws affecting collective bargaining, employee drug-testing, and the American with Disabilities Act, are now included in the Regulatory Quality Index and merged into the general economic regulation category. Fifth, the OECD index used in the Crain (2005) estimate of economic regulations did not cover all business sectors.

In summary, the methodology for estimating the cost of economic regulations is the main difference between this report and prior reports. This improvement is made possible because of new research at the World Bank to measure economic regulations. This Regulatory Quality Index is available for a larger number of countries and for a longer sample period than anything available for prior studies. More important, the Regulatory Quality Index embodies extensive stakeholder knowledge about the countries' regulatory practices that affect domestic and international practices that are related to product markets and labor markets.

Cross-Country Regression Model

The cost of economic regulations is derived from regression analysis using a panel of OECD member countries, which includes the United States. The basic idea is to estimate empirically the impact of regulations on aggregate economic output, or GDP. The approach uses the Regulatory Quality Index as the main variable of interest, while controlling for other variables that affect national economic performance. The form of the regression model is specified in Equation 1.

$$\text{GDP per Capita}_{It} = \beta\,(\text{World Bank Index of Regulatory Quality})_{It} + \phi\,(X)_{It} + \alpha_i + \varepsilon_{It} \qquad \text{(Eq. 1)}$$

The sample used to estimate Equation (1) consists of 25 OECD countries for which data on all of the relevant variables are available. The variable subscript *i* in Equation (1) denotes an observation in a particular country *i* (= 1, ..,25). The variable subscript *t* denotes an observation in a particular year, where *t* = 2002 through 2008.[23]

The dependent variable, GDP per capita, is real GDP divided by population, denominated in constant U.S. dollars (source: World Bank, 2010). The main explanatory variable of interest in Equation (1) is the *World Bank Regulatory Quality Index* (source: World Bank, 2009). This *Regulatory Quality Index* is scaled to have values that range from -2.5 to 2.5. Note that increases correspond to improvements in regulatory quality — that is, reductions in the regulatory burden imposed on the operation of product and factor markets.

The model also includes several economic and demographic control variables, represented by the vector *X* in Equation (1). These control variables are drawn from the empirical literature that examines differences in economic levels across countries and over time. (For useful surveys of this literature, see Hall and Jones, 1997, Barro and Sala-i-Martin, 1995, and Barro, 1997.) The set of controls included in *X* are: foreign trade as a share of GDP, country population, primary school enrollment as a share of the eligible population, and fixed broadband subscribers per 100 people (data source: World Bank, World Development Indicators, online database). The variables are entered into the regression model as natural logarithmic transformations.

Because the dataset is organized as a panel — that is, it includes observations over time for the same set of countries — the model also includes country fixed-effects variables. Fixed-effects variables are simply country-specific indicator variables that control for time-invariant factors that affect economic performance. For example, a landlocked country may be disadvantaged relative to a country with ocean access. Geographic location obviously does not change over time, and including the fixed-effects variables helps to control for the impact of such factors. Appendix Table A-2 provides summary statistics for the variables used in the analysis.

The results of estimating Equation 1 are shown in Table 2, and these parameters are used to calibrate the cost of economic regulations.

As reported in Table 2, the coefficient on the World Bank *Regulatory Quality Index* is positive and significant at the one-percent confidence level. This indicates that less stringent restrictions systematically enhance a country's aggregate economic activity, as reflected by the level of its GDP per capita. The estimated coefficient is 0.094. This means that a one-unit change in the *Regulatory Quality Index* corresponds to a 9.4 percent change in real GDP per capita (recall that the dependent variable is entered into the regression model as a logarithmic transformation and thus percentage changes).[24] The Regulatory Quality Index value for the United States is equal to 1.579 in 2008, and, as noted, the index is calibrated to range between -2.5 and 2.5. The difference between 1.579 and 2.5 (the minimal amount of regulation) would require a change equal to 0.92, which would correspond to an increase in U.S. GDP per capita of 8.7 percent (=0.094 x 0.92). The estimated cost of economic regulations as reflected in lost GDP in 2008 is thus $1.236 trillion (denominated in 2009 dollars).

This estimated cost represents a very large increase over the estimated cost of economic regulations in 2004, which equaled $671 billion after converting the estimate in Crain (2005) into 2009 dollars.

As noted, some of this difference is attributable to the change in the cost accounting methodology, one that is more complete than methodologies used in the prior studies for SBA.

The 2008 estimate includes labor market economic regulations that were included under the "workplace regulations" category in the 2004 estimate. The approximate value of the "economic" component of the workplace regulations category in 2004 is $56 billion (again adjusting for inflation).

Table 2. Impact of Economic Regulations on GDP in OECD Countries, 2002 through 2008

Independent Variable	ln (GDP per Capita) [a]
World Bank Regulatory Quality Index	0.094
	(2.77)**
ln (Country Population)	0.089
	(0.39)
ln (Foreign Trade as a Share of GDP)	0.242
	(4.95)**
ln (Primary Education as a Share of the Eligible Population)	-0.243
	(-2.37)*
ln (Fixed broadband subscribers per 100 people)	0.032
	(8.89)**
Constant	8.31
	(2.19)*
Observations	118
Number of Countries	25
R-square Within	0.85
R-square Between	0.03
F-stat (6,87)	85.4**

Notes to Table 2: t-statistics in parentheses where:
* indicates significance at the 5 percent confidence level.
** indicates significance at the 1 percent confidence level.
The variables are denominated in 2009 U.S. dollars. The model includes fixed- country effects and fixed-year effects when significant.

This means that the comparable economic regulations cost (one that includes product and labor market regulations) in 2004 is $727 billion (=$671+$56). Even after readjustment to account for the redefined categories, this still suggests that economic regulations increased by 70 percent from 2004 to 2008, or roughly $500 billion.

How much of this large increase comes from "real" regulatory changes and how much comes from methodological changes? If the cost of economic regulations in 2004 is re-estimated using the new methodology, that value rises by $445 billion to $1.172 trillion. This recalibration of the 2004 estimate suggests that the "real" cost of economic regulations increased by $63 billion between 2004 and 2008, after adjusting for inflation and estimation methods.

2. Environmental Regulations

Cost estimates for environmental regulations are derived from two sources: OMB's annual reports to Congress and Hahn and Hird (1991). The report assumes that OMB's coverage of environmental regulations has been relatively complete. OMB has reviewed the regulatory impact analyses for the most costly regulations promulgated by the Environmental Protection Agency back through the late 1980s. In its reports, OMB has relied on the cost estimates in Hahn and Hird (1991) to gauge the costs of environmental regulations prior to 1988, and this study follows that procedure.[25]

Table 3 lists the sources and estimated annual costs for environmental regulations that were enacted during various time periods. It is important to stress that the costs of environmental regulations shown in Table 3 are denominated in 2001 dollars, the same base year used in the original OMB sources of these estimates. This facilitates comparisons to the OMB reports, and these costs are converted into 2009 dollars in Section IV below.

OMB discusses the shortcomings in these estimates, including the basic fact that cost estimates do not exist for all environmental regulations, and the inherent difficulties in performing the regulatory impact analyses (RIAs). For example, OMB does not include an estimate for the cost of the Superfund program, which is likely to be quite large. To account for some of these shortcomings, OMB provides a range of cost estimates for most regulations, and these are reported in Table 3.

Beginning in its 2003 report, OMB began the practice of limiting its cost summaries to regulations promulgated over the preceding 10 years, which in that report covered 1992 through mid-2002.[26] For this reason, this report begins with the OMB report for 2001, which includes its earliest cost accounting and takes Hahn and Hird (1991) as its beginning estimate of the costs prior to 1988. To account for environmental regulations promulgated since then, the costs of newly reviewed regulations are taken from OMB's annual reports for 2002 through 2009.

Table 3. Sources and Estimated Annual Costs of Environmental Regulations

Years Regulations Were Issued *	Cost Estimates (Millions of 2001 $)		Source for Estimate
	Low	High	
Through 2000, Q1	108,359	191,887	OMB 2001, Table 2
Apr 1999 to Sep 2001	11,380	12,812	OMB 2002, Table 7
Oct 2001 to Sep 2002	192	192	OMB 2003, Table 1
Oct 2002 to Sep 2003	335	335	OMB 2004, Table 1
Oct 2003 to Oct 2004	3,840	4,073	OMB 2005, Table 1-1
Oct 2004 to Sep 2005	2,609	3,373	OMB 2006, Table 1-3
Oct 2005 to Sep 2006	2,720	2,965	OMB 2007, Table 1-3
Oct 2006 to Sep 2007	7,475	7,584	OMB 2008, Table 1-3
Oct 2007 to Sep 2008	7,591	8,780	OMB 2009, Table 1-3
Total	144,501	232,001	

Note to Table 3: These dates follow OMB's practice by reporting the costs by fiscal years, which begin October 1 and end September 30.

As shown in Table 3, this puts the cost of environmental regulations in a range between $144 billion and $232 billion (in 2001 dollars) or between $175 billion and $280 billion when converted into 2009 dollars. This report uses the high end of the cost range provided in the OMB reports and Hahn and Hird (1991). This reflects a judgment that cost estimates are absent for important environmental regulations and that government agencies tend to be conservative in estimating regulatory costs.[27] For comparison, if the midpoint of the high and low estimates were used, the cost of environmental regulations in this report would decline by roughly $50 billion, or 19 percent.

3. Tax Compliance

Prior studies of federal regulations stress the substantial burden of paperwork costs on the American public and businesses. In the modern era in which electronic submissions are displacing paper, the term *"paperwork burden"* has become merely a metaphor for the time and resources required for monitoring, recordkeeping, reporting, and compliance with statutes and regulations. Of this burden, the time required to comply with the federal tax code accounts for the lion's share. Of course, the federal government requires a host of additional forms that also impose recordkeeping and reporting burdens. However, these non-tax-related reporting and compliance requirements are largely tied to specific economic, environmental, or occupational safety and health and homeland security regulations. This means that the cost estimates for the other regulations will account for most of the non-tax-related compliance and reporting burden. In that sense, a separate estimate would be double-counting recordkeeping and form filing costs.

The estimates of the cost of federal tax compliance in prior studies for Advocacy relied mostly on annual studies of tax compliance produced by the Tax Foundation. These studies provided extensive details about the time required to file federal income tax forms and the number of specific forms filed. The estimates in this report rely mostly on data directly available from the U.S. Internal Revenue Service, simply because the Tax Foundation's latest report was for 2005. For certain forms, the Tax Foundation's estimates of the time required to file in 2005 are used.

The estimate of tax compliance costs in 2008 is consistent with past reports for Advocacy and is easy to describe. The first step compiles data from the Internal Revenue Service and in some cases from the Tax Foundation on the amount of time required to complete each type of tax form, and the number of filings for each type of form. The number of compliance hours is shown in the first row of Table 4 broken down by businesses and by individual and nonprofits, with a total for these two categories. The total number of hours required for compliance is nearly 4.3 billion per year, with businesses devoting about 2.3 billion hours and individuals and nonprofits devoting about 2.0 billion hours.

Table 4. Sources and Estimated Costs of Compliance with the Federal Tax Code

	Businesses	Individuals and Nonprofits	Total
# Hours Required to Comply	2,280,966,382	2,018,119,637	4,299,086,018
Compliance Cost per Hour (in 2009 $)	$ 49.77	$ 31.53	
Total Compliance Cost (in 2009 $)	$95,984,291,402	$ 63,635,262,186	$ 159,619,553,588
Share of Total Compliance Cost	60%	40%	

The second step is to multiply the hours spent on compliance by an hourly wage rate that reflects either the value of the preparer's time (the average hourly wage rate for accountant and auditors in the case of individuals and nonprofits) or the hourly compensation rate for Human Resources professionals (in the case of businesses).[28] The estimated cost of federal tax compliance is nearly $160 billion (in 2009 dollars). To be clear, this $160 billion estimate includes the combined costs on individual filers, nonprofit organizations, and business filers. The estimated cost of compliance for businesses is about $96 billion, accounting for 60 percent of the total cost.

4. Occupational Safety and Health and Homeland Security Regulations

Prior studies for Advocacy used "workplace regulations" as one of the four categories for analysis. This category covered a wide array of regulations dealing with wages, benefits, safety and health, and civil rights, among other things.[29] Because the economic cost component of workplace regulations is now reclassified and scored under the "economic" regulations category, this report modifies the workplace category to include only workplace regulations that deal with safety and health. These are primarily issued by the Occupational Safety and Health Administration, a division of the U.S. Department of Labor.

Table 5. Sources and Estimated Costs of Occupational Safety and Health and Homeland Security Regulations

Type of Workplace Regulation	Cost Estimate (Millions of 2009 $)	Source
Occupational Safety and Health (for those issued pre-2001)	64,313	Johnson (2005)
Occupational Safety and Health (for those issued 2001-2008)	471	OMB (2009), Table 1-2
Homeland Security (all through 2008)	10,416	OMB (2009), p. 18
Total	75,200	

It is noteworthy that occupational safety and health regulations alone accounted for 53 percent of the compliance costs of all workplace regulations in the 2005 study (Crain 2005). These were by far the largest element within the workplace regulations category.

This report relies on three sources to estimate the costs of occupational safety and health and homeland security regulations. These costs and sources are summarized in Table 5.

The cost calculations from the Johnson (2005) study are used where possible, that is, until 2001, and adjusted for inflation as shown in Table 5. The costs provided by OMB on OSHA regulations are used for those regulations issued subsequent to the Johnson study. All 17 of the homeland security regulations included in this report have been implemented since the 2005 report for Advocacy, and these cost estimates are all taken from OMB (2009). As examples, these are regulations concerned with transportation facilities security, chemical plant security, electronic availability of passenger manifest lists, cargo security, notice of imported food and registration of food facilities that might be vulnerable to bioterrorism, and air cargo security. The cost of these 17 homeland security regulations is $10.4 billion, and the total cost for this category — Occupational Safety and Health plus Homeland Security — is $75.2 billion.

Table 6. Summary of Regulatory Compliance Costs in 2008 (Billions of 2009 dollars)

Type of Regulation	Cost Estimate	Sources
All Federal Regulations	1,752	Summation of Costs by Type
Economic	1,236	Original regression analysis using World Bank Regulatory Quality Index
Environmental	281	Hahn and Hird (1991); Crain (2005); OMB (2004, 2005, 2006, 2007, 2008, 2009)
Tax Compliance	160	IRS website, Bureau of Labor Statistics; Tax Foundation (2005)
Occupational Safety and Health, and Homeland Security	75	Johnson (2005); OMB (2009)

Summary of Total Regulatory Costs

Table 6 summarizes the cost estimates described in this section by regulatory category, and notes the basic sources and procedures behind the estimates.

III. INCIDENCE OF REGULATORY COSTS

This section describes how the burden of federal regulations is distributed among major business sectors of the American economy, and, within sectors, how this burden is distributed among firms of different sizes. It begins with a brief quantitative summary of the composition of American enterprise: how the number of firms and the work force are distributed among firms of different sizes and among the major categories of business activities. This underlying composition of economic activity in America is a key element in the study, because it provides the basis for determining the incidence of regulatory costs.

A Snapshot of American Enterprise

The report uses a three-part firm size classification, relying on data available from Advocacy on employees per firm:

- Small firms — fewer than 20 employees
- Medium-sized firms — 20 to 499 employees
- Large firms — 500 or more employees

The North American Industry Classification System (NAICS) devised by the U.S. Census Bureau divides American businesses into 2,000 distinct industry types. In order to make the results tractable, this report distills these classifications down to five broad categories:

- Manufacturing,
- Trade (wholesale and retail trade),
- Services,
- Health care, and
- Other (a residual containing almost all other nonfarm employers).[30]

Four of these five categories are adopted from the original Hopkins (1995) study for Advocacy. The health care category was added in the Crain (2005) study for Advocacy to reflect the growing scale and importance of this sector within the U.S. economy. The rationale for a small number of large categories, here and in previous reports for Advocacy, is to gain insight into the distribution of the regulatory burden across various types of economic activity—"manufacturing" versus "services" provides an obvious and distinct boundary. The "other" category includes: forestry, fishing, hunting and agriculture, mining, utilities, construction, and transportation and warehousing. To be sure, "other" bundles a diverse set of economic activities into a single category. However, in creating additional sector categories the analysis becomes less tractable.

Table 7 shows the distribution of American industry by sector and firm size using the most recently available data (for 2006) from Advocacy.[31] Table 7 presents three relevant size indicators: the number of firms, the number of employees, and payroll expenditures.[32] For example, the data indicate some six million firms in the United States and roughly 5.4 million of these are small businesses (less than 20 employees).

Table 8 reports these business size indicators in a slightly different format, as shares of all U.S. industry, which are used to allocate compliance costs. Table 8 simply converts the raw data shown in Table 7 into percentage terms. For example, consider the data in Table 8 that describe the manufacturing sector. Manufacturing accounts for 5 percent of all U.S. firms, 11 percent of all U.S. employment, and 13 percent of all U.S. business payroll expenditures. Within the manufacturing sector, 75 percent of the firms are classified as small businesses (fewer than 20 employees), 24 percent have between 20 and 499 employees, and only one percent has 500 or more employees.

Nine percent of manufacturing employees work in small firms, 36 percent in mid-sized firms, and 56 percent in large firms. Finally, regarding the distribution of payroll expenditures, small firms account for 7 percent, mid-sized firms account for 31 percent, and large firms account for 62 percent.

The percentages displayed in Table 8 provide a snapshot of the distribution of productive activity and resources among broad sectors of American industry. It is against this descriptive backdrop that the report charts the incidence of regulatory compliance costs. These costs are allocated across the sectors and firm sizes shown in Table 8 using the procedures described in the remainder of this section.

Table 7. Size Distribution of American Business in 2006*

Sector	Size Measure	All Firms [a]	Firm Size: <20 Employees	20-499 Employees	500+ Employees
All Sectors [a]	Firms	6,022,127	5,377,631	626,425	18,071
	Employment	119,917,165	21,609,520	38,614,220	59,693,425
	Payroll ($000)	5,099,088,373	772,519,440	1,492,491,07	2,834,077,86
Manufacturing	Firms	278,703	210,220	66,890	1,593
	Employment	13,631,683	1,180,832	4,875,389	7,575,462
	Payroll ($000)	659,910,538	44,023,629	205,977,710	409,909,200
Trade	Firms	1,048,443	941,506	105,527	1,410
	Employment	21,798,513	4,060,460	5,939,480	11,798,573
	Payroll ($000)	35,798,406	128,105,755	238,874,376	368,818,276
Services	Firms	3,064,433	2,755,361	296,335	12,738
	Employment	55,026,464	10,386,251	17,413,803	27,346,941
	Payroll ($000)	2,420,355,343	354,457,788	627,515,860	1,427,510,87
Health Care	Firms	596,992	526,261	69,895	835
	Employment	16,451,361	2,544,976	5,401,418	8,504,967
	Payroll ($000)	666,681,058	112,830,630	186,810,745	367,039,682
Other	Firms	1,033,556	944,284	87,778	1,494
	Employment	13,009,144	3,430,737	4,982,216	4,634,181
	Payroll ($000)	616,343,027	132,247,939	231,835,480	250,237,452

Notes to Table 7.*

Source: U.S. Small Business Administration, Office of Advocacy, "Statistics of U.S. Businesses: Firm Size Data," website: http://www.sba.gov /advo/stats/data.html. Payroll data are converted into 2009 dollars. The Office of Advocacy contracts with the U.S. Census Bureau to provide employer firm size data. These data for 2006 are the most recently available from the SBA.

[a] These Statistics of U.S. Businesses data cover almost all nonfarm employer businesses. Omitted are farms, railroads, and most government-owned establishments, the U.S. Postal Service, and large pension, health, and welfare funds (100 + employees) and nonincorporated firms with no paid employees.

Table 8. Size Distribution of American Business (As a Percentage of Private Industry Employment)

	Sector Share of All U.S. Industry					
Size Measure	Manufacturing	Trade	Services	Health Care	Other	
No. of Firms	5	17	51	10	17	
Employees	11	18	46	14	11	
Annual Payroll	13	14	47	13	12	
	Percent of Firms, by Sector					
	Manufacturing	Trade	Services	Health Care	Other	All Sectors
<20 employees	75	90	90	88	91	89
20-499 employees	24	10	10	12	9	10
500+ employees	1	0.1	0.4	0.1	0.1	0.3
	Percent of Employees, by Sector					
	Manufacturing	Trade	Services	Health Care	Other	All Sectors
<20 employees	9	19	19	15	26	18
20-499 employees	36	27	32	33	38	32
500+ employees	56	54	50	52	36	50
	Percent of Payroll, by Sector					
	Manufacturing	Trade	Services	Health Care	Other	All Sectors
<20 employees	7	17	15	17	21	15
20-499 employees	31	32	26	28	38	29
500+ employees	62	50	59	55	41	56

Source: See Table 7.

Assumptions and Procedures Underlying the Cost Allocations

Business Portion of the Regulatory Burden

Before costs can be allocated across these five business sectors, a more general cost allocation is necessary, specifically how much of the regulatory burden falls in the aggregate on businesses. This task requires a delineation of the regulatory burden that falls initially on business from the burden that falls initially on individuals and state and local governments. As discussed in Section II, the report does not attempt to map out the subsequent shifting of this burden from businesses to individuals (*e.g.*, in the form of higher retail prices) or from one business sector to another (*e.g.*, in the form of higher energy prices or health insurance premiums). It is worth emphasizing that all regulatory costs are — and can only be — borne by individuals, as consumers, as workers, as stockholders, as owners, or as taxpayers. In other words, the distinction between "business" and "individual" is one that focuses on the compliance responsibility, fully recognizing that ultimately all costs must fall on individuals. Moreover, the degree to which businesses are able to shift compliance costs forward onto consumers can only be determined with highly specific information about the market elasticities. For example, without the price elasticity of demand, we cannot determine with any level of certainty what percentage of the regulatory cost will be shifted forward beyond the statutory incidence.

A second rationale for attempting to apportion costs between businesses and individuals is that the incidence of costs across different sectors of the economy is potentially quite important from a policy perspective, and the consumer costs cannot be allocated to the different classes of businesses. As a final introductory comment, some of the costs of federal regulations fall on state and local governments. Homeland security regulations are a good example of such costs. These costs borne by state and local governments are bundled with those borne by individuals to keep a relatively tractable division in business versus non business costs.

The cost allocations for each type of regulation are shown in Table 9.

The allocations shown in Table 9 generally employ the same methodology used in Hopkins (1995), and Crain and Hopkins (2001), and Crain (2005). The allocation of environmental regulations is based on the compliance data reported by the Environmental Protection Agency.[33]

Table 9. Allocation of Compliance Cost Incidence to Business

Type of Regulation	Business Incidence (% of Category Costs)	Other Incidence (% of Category Costs)
Economic	50	50
Environmental	65	35
Tax Compliance	60	40
Occupational Safety and Health, and Homeland Security	97	3

In the absence of allocation data for economic regulation, a default judgment of 50-50 is applied. The allocation for federal tax compliance uses the apportionment data from the IRS as shown in Table 4. Occupational Safety and Health, and Homeland Security are allocated 97 percent to businesses and 3 percent to other. This assumption is consistent with the empirical evidence that the labor supply function is relatively inelastic, and therefore safety and health costs are not immediately shifted onto consumers.[34] The assumption is that a small share (3 percent) of estimated homeland security costs is borne by state and local governments and individuals.

Allocation of Regulatory Costs Across Business Sectors

The second task is to allocate the business portion of regulatory costs among the five major sectors. These five sectors generally follow those in Hopkins (1995), Crain and Hopkins (2001), and Crain (2005) to facilitate comparisons over time. The sectors are based on the Census Bureau's North American Industry Classification System (NAICS), in some cases aggregating categories.[35]

Table 10. Allocation of Business Regulatory Costs to Sectors (Percentages)

Type of Regulation	Sectoral Allocations					Sources and Summary of Methods
	Manufac-turing	Trade	Services	Health Care	Other	
Economic	12	18	46	13	11	BEA (Value added share of private GDP); SBA (Employment share of private workforce)
Environmental	54	0	0.3	1	45	Hazilla and Kopp, 1991 (Compliance Costs by Sector)
Tax Compliance	3	14	58	7	17	IRS, Statistics of Income (Sector share of total returns filed, weighted by cost of filings)
Occupational Safety and Health, and Homeland Security	14	18	49	12	8	SBA (Employment share of private workforce); BEA (Value added share of private GDP)

For example, the NAICS separates wholesale trade and retail trade, and these are combined in this report. Table 10 lists these allocations by sector and the sources and methods used. A more complete description of the allocation basis for each type of regulation is described in turn.

Economic Regulations

Regarding economic regulations, the cost allocations are based on a weighted average of two components: (i) the sector's value added to GDP divided by total private sector GDP, and (ii) the number of employees on the sector divided by total private sector employment. [36] The average for each sector is weighted by the share of non-OSHA workplace regulations on the sector. That is, a sector's employment share gets a slightly higher weight where regulations such as "labor standards" or "labor management relations" are likely to have a larger impact.

Environmental Regulations

The sector allocations for environmental regulations are taken from Hazilla and Kopp.[37] Almost all of these costs fall on the manufacturing sector (54 percent) and the "other" sector (45 percent). The "other" sector includes such businesses as coal mining, ore mining, oil and gas extraction, coal gasification, and electric utilities, all of which are heavily affected by regulations promulgated under the Clean Air Act and the Clean Water Act. The remaining one percent of environmental costs falls on the health care and service sectors.

Federal Tax Compliance

The allocation of federal tax compliance costs is derived from IRS Statistics of Income data that indicate the number of returns and forms filed by each type of business by sector, sole proprietorships, partnerships, and corporations. These data are summarized in Table 11.

Occupational Safety and Health, and Homeland Security Regulations

The costs of homeland security regulations are allocated based on each sector's share of value added to private sector GDP. The costs of occupational safety and health regulations are allocated based on each sector's share of private sector employment. The sum of these two sector costs then determines the overall sector share.

Table 11. Cost Allocation for Federal Tax Compliance

	Sole Proprietorship	Partnerships	Corporations	All Businesses	
Total Number of Returns / Forms Filed	39,503,733	3,445,433	6,922,433	49,871,600	
Share of Forms:					
Manufacturing	2%	2%	5%		
Trade	12%	8%	18%		
Services	56%	80%	52%		
Health Care	9%	2%	8%		
Other	22%	9%	18%		
Compliance Costs (in Millions of 2009 $):					Cost Share
Manufacturing	475	289	2,417	3,181	3%
Trade	3,642	1,335	8,451	13,429	14%
Services	16,943	13,991	24,871	55,805	58%
Health Care	2,645	409	3,819	6,874	7%
Other	6,626	1,520	8,549	16,695	17%

Allocation of Regulatory Costs by Firm Size

The third task of this study involves allocating the costs of regulations by firm size. As noted above, this study adopts a three-division scheme: firms with fewer than 20 employees ("small"), firms with 20 to 499 employees ("medium," or "mid-sized"), and firms with 500 or more employees ("large"). The specific allocation procedure differs for each type of regulation, and the procedures are described below.

Starting with economic regulations, the cost allocation among the three firm size groups uses a two-step procedure. Step one seeks to separate the total regulatory costs for the sector into two components, those that apply to all firms and those that explicitly exempt small firms (those with fewer than 20 employees). In step two, for the nonexempt regulations, the procedure follows Crain and Hopkins (2001) and Crain (2005) and allocates these costs based on the share of payroll expenditure within each firm size category (shown in Table 8 above). For example, in the manufacturing sector, small firms generate 7 percent of payroll within the sector, medium-sized firms generate 31 percent, and large firms generate 62 percent. This procedure is used because payroll expenditures are the best available proxy for the economic activity by firm size. The portion of economic regulations from which small firms are exempt is approximated using the share of costs that were exempt in the Johnson 2005 study. This historical share is then multiplied by the currently estimated cost of economic regulations to estimate exempted costs. These exempted costs are then reallocated to the medium- sized and large firms based on their respective employment shares. In other words, the aggregate costs of economic regulations include some regulations that exempt small firms and these exempted costs are reapportioned to mid-sized and large firms. The costs reapportioned to mid-sized and large firms are sector-specific, and based on the relative employment shares by firm size in each sector.

The methodology used to allocate the cost of environmental regulations by firm size is described in detail in Appendix 5 and is relatively easy to summarize. The procedure uses multiple regression analysis to estimate the relationship between pollution abatement costs (PAC) per employee and firm size, measured by the number of employees per firm. The model regresses firm compliance costs per employee against the number of employees, controlling for other factors. The regression results indicate that a 1 percent increase in firm size (measured in terms of the number of employees) corresponds to a 0.43 percent decrease in pollution abatement costs per employee. In essence, this parameter estimates the degree of economies of scale in compliance costs.

This "economies of scale" parameter value is used to solve for the median cost per employee within each firm size category for each business sector. To state the problem differently, given the economies of scale parameter and the share of employees within each size class, what per-employee cost for the three firm size classes would yield the overall sector average cost? Other studies are consistent with this finding of economies of scale in environmental regulatory compliance, although Becker (2005) finds that economies of scale differ depending on the type of pollutant.[38]

The allocation of tax compliance costs across the firm sizes starts with the information reported in Table 11, the compliance costs by sector and by type on business (sole proprietorships, partnerships, and corporations). Within each sector, the following apportionment strategy is used. All of the costs for sole proprietorships are allocated to small businesses. The costs for partnerships are distributed between small and mid-sized businesses based on their shares of payroll expenditures. For example, consider the manufacturing sector. Of total payroll spending by small firms and midsized firms, small firms account for 17 percent and mid-sized firms account for 83 percent. Thus, 17 percent of the compliance costs for manufacturing partnerships are allocated to small businesses and 83 percent to mid-sized businesses. Similarly, the compliance costs for corporations are distributed between mid-sized and large businesses based on their shares of payroll expenditures. Again using the example of the manufacturing sector, of total payroll spending by mid-sized firms and large firms, mid-sized firms account for 31 percent and large firms account for 69 percent. Thus, 31 percent of the compliance costs for manufacturing corporations are allocated to midsized businesses and 69 percent to large businesses.

The costs of occupational safety and health, and homeland security regulations are distributed among the three firm size categories such that the cost per employee in small firms is 20 percent higher than in medium-sized firms, and the cost per employee in large firms is 20 percent lower than in medium-sized firms. For the regulations that exempt small firms, the costs are allocated solely between the medium-sized and large firms using the same ratio as above (20 percent lower per employee in large firms than in medium-sized firms). The final allocation then sums the nonexempt and exempt cost components for each firm size category.[39]

IV. Principal Findings

This section presents the report's principal findings regarding the total cost of federal regulations and the distribution of this cost across major sectors of the economy, and across firms of different sizes.

A Preliminary Benchmark: Total Federal Regulatory Costs per Household

One way to illustrate the magnitude of the total cost of federal regulations is in relation to the number of U.S. households. Table 12 presents this cost per household data as a benchmark for comparing how the regulatory burden has changed over time based on the previous studies for Advocacy. However, it is important to caution the reader that this particular benchmark includes the total cost of regulations and makes no effort to distinguish between how much of this cost falls on individuals compared with businesses. It simply assumes that households (as consumers, workers, small business owners, shareholders, and so on) ultimately bear the entire burden of regulations. Further, as noted throughout this report, the estimation methodologies have evolved since the initial study in 1995, and, obviously, this accounts for some of the differences in costs. Table 12 also shows the total federal government burden, encompassing federal tax receipts, and how this total burden per household changed during this time period. The data in Table 12 are adjusted for inflation and expressed in 2009 dollars.

Table 12. Federal Regulatory Costs and Federal Receipts per Household (HH), Compared to Prior Studies for the Office of Advocacy [a]

Year	Households (Millions)	Total Regulatory Costs per HH	Federal Receipts per HH [b]	Combined Federal Burden per HH
2008	112	$15,586	$ 22,375	$ 37,962
2004	109	$ 11,550 [c]	$ 19,516	$ 27,359
2000	106	$ 10,362 [d]	$ 23,903	$ 30,176
1995	98	$ 9,580 [e]	$ 19,309	$ 25,441
Avg. Annual Growth Rate: 1995 to 2008	1.1%	4.8%	1.2%	2.4%

Notes to Table 12:

[a] All dollar amounts are adjusted for inflation and denominated in 2009 dollars.

[b] Federal receipts by fiscal years, including Social Security. Source: CBO Web Site: http://www.cbo.gov/showdoc.cfm?index=1821&sequence=0.

[c] Source: Crain (2005).

[d] Source: Crain and Hopkins (2001). As described in Crain (2005) this estimate for 2000 adjusts the cost originally reported in Crain and Hopkins (2001) upward by $37 billion to be consistent and comparable with the calculation methods and sources introduced in the Crain (2005) report.

[e] Source: Hopkins (1995).

As shown in Table 12, the total cost of federal regulations per household reached $15,586 in 2008, an increase of more than $4,000 per household since 2004 after adjusting for inflation. (A substantial portion of the 2004-2008 increase shown in Table 12 is the result of the change in methodology in the calculation of the costs estimate for economic regulation). The combined federal burden — federal receipts plus regulatory costs — reached $37,962 per household in 2008, an increase since 2004 of nearly $6,900 per household. The combined federal burden is growing at a real annual rate of 5.5 percent. An interesting observation in Table 12 is the sharp increase in growth rates in comparison to the 2000 to 2004 period. In that four-year period, the combined federal burden per household fell at annual rate of 2.3 percent.

Distribution of Federal Regulatory Costs: Businesses and Others

Table 13 shows the estimated costs of all federal regulations, broken down by type, and the distribution of the burden between businesses and others (*i.e.*, individuals and state and local governments).

Table 13. Total Cost of Federal Regulations in 2008 by Type and Business Share (Billions of 2009 Dollars)

		Business Portion		Others	
	Total Costs (Billions of $)	Share (Percent)	Amount (Billions of $)	Share (Percent)	Amount (Billions of $)
All Federal Regulations	1,752	55%	970	45%	782
Economic	1,236	50%	618	50%	618
Environmental	281	65%	183	35%	98
Tax Compliance	160	60%	96	40%	64
Occupational Safety and Health, and Homeland Security	75	97%	73	3%	2

These estimates in Table 13 indicate that the annual total cost of all federal regulations in 2008 was $1.752 trillion. Of this amount, the annual direct burden on business is $970 billion. Economic regulations represent the most costly category, with a total cost of $1.236 trillion, and with $618 billion falling initially on business. Environmental regulations represent the second most costly category in terms of total cost ($281 billion), and the cost apportioned to business is $183 billion. Compliance with the federal tax code is the third most costly category ($160 billion), and the cost of occupational safety and health, and homeland security regulations ranks last ($75 billion).

Table 14. Average Sectoral Regulatory Costs, 2008 (In 2009 Dollars) Total Costs

	Billions of Dollars)	Cost per Firm (Dollars)	Cost per Employee (Dollars)	Cost as a Share of Payroll (Percent)
		Manufacturing		
Total	193	688,194	14,070	29
Economic	82	293,660	6,004	12
Environmental	98	352,689	7,211	15
Tax Compliance	3	11,415	233	0.5
OSHHS *	8	30,431	622	2
		Trade		
Total	115	109,970	5,289	16
Economic	89	84,811	4,079	12
Environmental	-	-	-	-
Tax Compliance	13	12,808	616	2
OSHHS *	13	12,351	594	2
		Services		
Total	400	129,912	7,235	15
Economic	308	100,460	5,595	13
Environmental	1	177	10	0
Tax Compliance	56	18,211	1,014	2
OSHHS *	35	11,065	616	1
		Health Care		
Total	69	116,326	4,221	10
Economic	52	86,760	3,148	8
Environmental	1	2,056	75	0.2
Tax Compliance	7	11,514	418	1
OSHHS *	9	15,995	580	1
		Other		
Total	191	188,704	14,992	31
Economic	88	84,687	6,728	14
Environmental	83	79,900	6,348	13
Tax Compliance	17	16,153	1,283	3
OSHHS *	6	7,964	633	1
		U.S.Totals (All U.S. Businesses)		
Total	907	161,021	8,086	19
Economic	618	102,612	5,153	12
Environmental	183	30,329	1,523	4
Tax Compliance	96	15,939	800	2
OSHHS *	73	12,141	610	1

Note to Table 14:

* OSHHS stands for Occupational Safety and Health, and Homeland Security Regulations.

Distribution of the Regulatory Burden across Business Sectors: Three Metrics

Table 14 further deconstructs the business portion of regulatory costs by sector and by the four categories of regulations. Three measures of the regulatory burden are employed to assess the cost distribution among business sectors: cost per firm, cost per employee, and cost as a share of payroll expenses.

As shown in Table 14, considering all U.S. businesses and all federal regulations, the cost burden on the typical U.S. firm is about $161,000. The cost per employee for the typical U.S. firm tops $8,000. This cost of federal regulation in the typical U.S. firm equals 19 percent of payroll expenditures. To place this amount in perspective, it exceeds the employer contribution to the payroll tax for Social Security (OASDHI) and Medicare, which is 7.65 percent of wages. Indeed, 19 percent of payroll expenditures exceeds the combined payroll taxes for OASHDI and Medicare paid by employers and employees, or self-employed individuals, which equals 15.3 percent.

Table 15. Sector Rankings Based on Three Metrics of the Regulatory Burden (In 2009 Dollars. 1=highest burden; 5=lowest burden)

Business Sector	Cost Per Firm (Dollars)	Cost Per Firm (Rank)	Cost Per Employee (Dollars)	Cost Per Employee (Rank)	Cost /Payroll (Percent)	Cost /Payroll (Rank)
Manufacturing	688,944	1	14,070	2	29	2
Other	188,704	2	14,992	1	31	1
Services	129,912	3	7,235	3	15	4
Health Care	116,326	4	4,221	5	10	5
Trade	109,970	5	5,289	4	16	3

The three cost metrics described and shown in Table 14 reveal several noteworthy patterns in how the cost burden of regulations is distributed among the business sectors. Table 15 shows these patterns a bit more clearly by ranking the five sectors in terms of the relative cost burden.

As illustrated by the rankings in Table 15, the manufacturing sector and the "other" sector bear the largest regulatory burden by all three metrics. For example, using the "cost per firm" metric as a gauge, the distribution of the regulatory burden is heavily skewed toward these two sectors. The manufacturing sector in particular bears the highest total regulatory burden in terms of the average cost per firm. The burden on the manufacturing sector ($688,944 per manufacturing firm) exceeds the burden on the second most costly sector (the "other" category at $188,704 per firm) by a factor of 3.6. However, by the other two metrics — cost per employee and cost as a percent of payroll — the "other" category bears the highest burden. The cost per employee for firms in the "other" category is $14,992 as compared with the second highest sector (manufacturing), where the cost per employee is $14,070.

The difference between the rankings based on "cost per firm" versus "cost per employee" is likely explained by the fact that enterprises within these two sectors operate with different mixes of capital and labor. For example, predominant among the "other" category are utilities, mining (including coal and oil and gas extraction), and transportation and warehousing concerns, all of which require huge capital investments relative to the number of employees. This means that the regulatory cost per worker rises in this sector relative to manufacturing establishments that typically have more employees per unit of capital investment than establishments such as public utilities, airlines, and railroads. It is worth emphasis, however, that costs per employee in both of these sectors are double the cost per employee in the next highest-cost sector, services, where costs equal $7,235 per employee.

The second conclusion from the metrics in Table 15 is that regulatory costs are distributed much more evenly among the three remaining sectors: health care, services, and trade. For example, in terms of the cost per firm, the burden on the services sector is 12 percent higher than the health care sector and 18 percent higher than the trade sector. As a final observation, when the regulatory burden is gauged by "cost as a percent of payroll," the health care sector fares far better than any of the other sectors (equal to 10 percent). For example, the difference is large even compared to the second lowest cost industry, services, which equals 15 percent of payroll expenditures. Health care compliance costs as a share of payroll is one-third the level in the "other" sector.

In summary, some conclusions about the distribution of the regulatory burden among sectors depend on which metric one favors. However, the metrics uniformly indicate that the manufacturing sector and the "other" sector bear substantially higher regulatory costs compared with the services, health care, and trade sectors of the economy.

The Distribution of Regulatory Costs by Firm Size

The distribution of regulatory costs among different firm size categories is presented in Table 16.

Table 16. Regulatory Costs in Small, Medium-sized and Large Firms, 2008 (Cost per Employee in 2009 Dollars)

		Firm Size		
Type of Regulation	All Firms	<20	20-499	500
		Manufacturing		
Total	14,070	28,316	13,504	12,586
Economic	6,004	4,454	5,481	6,952
Environmental	7,211	22,594	7,131	4,865
Tax Compliance	233	444	205	219
OSHHS *	622	824	687	550
		Trade		
Total	5,289	5,453	6,242	4,753
Economic	4,079	3,673	4,866	3,823
Environmental	-	-	-	-
Tax Compliance	616	1,013	737	418
OSHHS *	594	767	639	511
		Services		
Total	7,235	7,106	6,274	7,815
Economic	5,595	4,181	4,668	6,648
Environmental	10	25	8	5
Tax Compliance	1,014	2,113	944	637
OSHHS *	616	786	655	524
		Health Care		
Total	4,221	5,375	3,707	4,204
Economic	3,148	3,318	2,725	3,366
Environmental	75	203	64	44
Tax Compliance	418	1,103	292	293
OSHHS *	633	772	643	514
		Other		
Total	14,992	21,906	12,878	11,964
Economic	6,728	5,273	6,700	7,721
Environmental	6,348	13,760	4,343	2,963
Tax Compliance	1,283	2,101	1,192	765
OSHHS *	633	772	643	514
		Total, All U.S. Businesses **		
Total	8,086	10,585	7,454	7,755
Economic	5,153	4,120	4,750	5,835
Environmental	1,523	4,101	1,294	883
Tax Compliance	800	1,584	760	517
OSHHS *	610	781	650	520

Notes for Table 16:

* OSHHS stands for Occupational Safety and Health, and Homeland Security Regulations

** The costs per employee for all U.S. Businesses are computed using the employment shares to weight the costs in each of the five respective sectors.

Considering first the aggregate costs for all federal regulations and all business sectors (displayed as the last category in Table 16), regulations cost small firms an estimated $10,585 per employee.[40] Regulations cost medium-sized firms $7,454 per employee, and large firms $7,755 per employee. Overall, the cost per employee is 42 percent higher in small compared with mid-sized firms, and 36 percent higher in small firms than in large firms. It is noteworthy that the distribution of costs across the three categories of firms in 2008 is similar to the findings in the prior study for Advocacy (Crain, 2005). In 2004 the cost differential between small and mid-sized firms was 41 percent; thus, the cost disadvantage to small businesses has remained nearly constant. In 2004 the cost differential between small and large firms was 45 percent, which is even greater than the gap estimated in 2008.

This suggests that since 2004, costs per employee have increased for large businesses relative to small and mid-sized businesses.[41]

Indeed, considering the costs of all regulations and all business sectors, mid-sized firms appear to have a slight advantage over large firms, and a wide advantage over small firm.

This pattern, however, is not uniform across sectors or types of regulations. As the results in Table 16 reveal, the distribution of compliance costs with respect to firm size classes differs across the five major business sectors. Indeed, even within sectors, the distribution of the burden varies with the type of regulation. Table 17 reports the percentage difference in the cost per employee in small firms versus larger firms by sector. That is, Table 17 restates the numbers in Table 16 in terms of the cost burden on small firms relative to mid-sized and large firms.

The disproportionate cost burden on small firms is dramatic for the manufacturing sector. In that sector the estimated cost per employee for small firms is 110 percent higher than in medium-sized firms ($28,316 versus $13,504), and 125 percent higher than in large firms ($28,316 versus $12,586). To drive home the importance of this result, in the U.S. manufacturing sector, small firms face a regulation burden that is more than double the burden faced by their larger rivals.

This cost disadvantage faced by small manufacturing firms appears in three of the four types of regulations (see the detailed breakdown by type of regulation in Table 16). The burden falls disproportionately on large manufacturing firms only in the case of economic regulations.[42] However, while some types of regulations disadvantage large firms relative to small, the combined impact of all regulations in the manufacturing sector puts small firms at a substantial competitive disadvantage.

The distribution of the regulatory burden among firms of different sizes in the "other" category is similar to that in the manufacturing sector, although the overall cost differentials are less extreme than in the manufacturing sector. The cost per employee is 70 percent higher in small firms than in medium-sized firms, and 83 percent higher in small firms than in large firms. The health care sector exhibits a similar disproportionate distribution. In that sector, the cost per employee is 45 percent higher in small firms than in medium-sized firms, and 28 percent higher in small firms than in large firms.

Table 17. Regulatory Costs in Small Firms Relative to Medium-sized and Large Firms in 2008 *

Business Sector	Small Firms Relative to Medium-Sized Firms	Small Firms Relative to Large Firms
Manufacturing	110	125
Trade	-13	15
Services	13	-9
Health Care	45	28
Other	70	83
All Sectors	42	36

* Note to Table 17:

The numbers reflect the percentage difference between regulatory costs per employee in a small firm versus a medium-sized firm or large firm using the data reported in Table 16.

The regulatory burden is distributed most evenly with respect to firm size in the services sector, as summarized in Table 17 and displayed in detail in Table 16. In the services sector the total cost per employee for small firms is only 13 percent larger than the cost in medium-sized firms, and 9 percent less than the cost in large firms. In the trade sector, small firms face a 15 percent heavier cost burden than large firms, but have a 13 percent cost advantage over medium-sized firms. In other words, within the trade sector, the heaviest cost burden falls on mid-sized firms.

Summary Comments

Overall and on almost every regulatory frontier, compliance costs place small businesses at a competitive disadvantage. The cost disadvantage confronting small business is driven by environmental regulations, tax compliance, and occupational safety and health and homeland security regulations. The particular cost drivers differ somewhat across the five business sectors, as the details of this report point out. Moreover, not all regulations fall more heavily on small firms than on their larger counterparts. For example, the cost of economic regulations falls most heavily on large firms in every sector except health care. The most disadvantaged of all by federal regulations are small manufacturing firms.

This study provides a broad sense of the costs of federal government regulations in the United States and how they affect the balance in public versus private sector responsibilities. In 2008 federal regulatory compliance absorbed about 14 percent of U.S. national income, a clear indication of what citizens give up in exchange for this government function.

APPENDIX 1. ELEMENTS INCLUDED IN THE WORLD BANK INDEX OF REGULATORY QUALITY AND DATA SUMMARY FOR ESTIMATING THE COSTS OF DOMESTIC ECONOMIC REGULATIONS

Table A-1. List of Concepts Included in the Regulatory Quality Index

Export and Import Regulations
Restrictions on ownership of business by non-residents
Restrictions on ownership of equity by non-residents
Unfair competitive practices
Price controls
Discriminatory tariffs
Excessive protections
Stock Exchange / Capital Markets
Foreign investment restrictions
Administrative regulations
Tax system is distortionary
Competition in local market is limited
Anti-monopoly policy is lax and ineffective

Complexity of tax system
Easy to start a company
Banking / finance restrictions
Wage and prices controls
Administrative business start-up formalities
Ease of market entry for new firms
Tax Effectiveness (How efficient the country's tax collection system is.) An assessment of whether the necessary business laws are in place. Labor Market Policies
Enabling Environment for Private Sector Development
How problematic are labor regulations for the growth of your business? How problematic are tax regulations for the growth of your business?
How problematic are custom and trade regulations for the growth of your business? Trade and foreign exchange system
Enabling conditions for rural financial services development
Investment climate for rural businesses
Access to agricultural input and produce markets
Banking regulation does not hinder competitiveness
Competition legislation in your country does not prevent unfair competition
Customs' authorities do not facilitate the efficient transit of goods
Financial institutions' transparency is not widely developed in your country
Labor regulations hinder business activities
Subsidies impair economic development

Source for Table A-1: Kaufmann, Daniel, Aart Kraay, and Massimo Mastruzzi (2009), Table B-4.

Table A-2. Summary Statistics for OECD Cross-Country Data Set

	mean	median	sd
GDP per Capita (in 2009 US $)	22,654	24,306	12,201
World Bank Index of Regulatory Quality	1.317	1.441	0.441
Population (in 1000s)	38,900	10,800	57,900
Fixed Broadband Subscribers per 100	14.2	13.3	10.1
Primary Education as a Share of the Eligible Population (times 100)	98	99	5
Foreign Trade as a Share of GDP (times	98	81	57

Appendix 2. Methodology Used to Correct Overcount of Firms in the SBA Data

When the Census Bureau compiles its Statistics of U.S. Businesses, it relies on survey questionnaires filled out by firms. Occasionally the firms classify themselves under more than one industry. Because some firms are redundantly classified, the sum of the firms within each category is actually greater than the entire number of firms.

To correct for this over count, the number of redundantly counted firms is calculated by summing the number of firms by industry and subtracting the total number of firms from this across-industry sum.

The next task is to assign a certain fraction of over counted firms to each industry to be used as a reduction factor. This is accomplished using the fact that the number of employees within each industry is accurately measured. Each industry's share of the total work force is calculated; these shares are then used to allocate the over counted firms to each industry. From there, it is a simple matter of subtracting the over count within each industry from the reported count in each industry. This ensures that the total number of firms is equal to the number of firms summed across the five industry categories.

Appendix 3. Methodology for Estimating Economies of Scale in Environmental Compliance Costs

Introduction

In 2008, environmental regulations cost an estimated $281 billion (16 percent of total federal regulatory costs), and the cost falling on businesses was an estimated $183 billion (19 percent of total business regulatory costs). This appendix describes the methodology used to estimate the relationship between firm size and compliance costs for environmental regulations. This methodology is adopted from Crain and Hopkins (2001) and Crain (2005), and the objective is to provide a basis for allocating the cost of environmental regulations among the three firm size categories.

The relationship between compliance costs and firm size is estimated using pollution abatement expenditures by manufacturing firms. For reasons described below the data used in the analysis are for 1992. Among environmental regulations, pollution abatement expenditures account for about one-fourth of the costs. Thus, a reliable estimate of scale economies in pollution abatement provides a reasonable approximation for the general distribution of all environmental regulatory costs.

Estimation Procedure and Results

The general approach is to estimate the relationship between pollution abatement cost (PAC) per employee and firm size, here measured by the number of employees per firm. Equation (2) specifies the estimation equation, which is estimated in log form:

$$\ln(\text{PAC / employee})_{i,s} = \beta \ln(\text{Firm Size}_{i,s}) + \phi \ln(\text{Value of Sales}_{i,s}) + \gamma_i + \varepsilon_{i,s} \quad \text{(Eq. 2)}$$

where subscript *i* stands for a specific industry type and subscript *s* stands for a specific American state. Industry types are defined by two-digit SIC codes covering all industries in the manufacturing sector; see Table A-8 below for a description of the 20 industries included. Each continuous variable is entered into Equation (2) as a natural logarithmic transformation (ln).

In Equation (2) the dependent variable, $(\text{PAC / employee})_{i,s}$, measures the average pollution abatement expenditure per employee in industry *i* in state *s* in 1994 (source: Bureau of the Census, 1996). These are the most recently available data, as Census no longer collects this series. These expenditure data include capital expenses and operating expenditures. The main independent variable of interest, firm size **i,s**, measures the average number of employees per firm in industry *i* in state *s* (source: Bureau of the Census, *1992 Economic Census*). The estimated coefficient on firm size, J3, thus provides the measure of economies of scale. Specifically, how does pollution abatement expenditure per employee respond to changes in firm size? Equation (2) also includes a control variable for the average value of sales, and a fixed-effects variable, **yi,** which seeks to control for other factors that cause pollution abatement costs to differ among the 20 industries. For example, the chemical industry may simply be subject to different environmental standards than, say, the leather products industry. Including the fixed-effects dummy variables in the model allows the cost function to shift for each specific industry. c **i,s** is the regression error term, which is assumed to be normally distributed.

Equation (2) is estimated across states using data for 1992. While the Census Bureau continued to survey pollution abatement expenditures through 1994, 1992 is used because the Census of Manufacturing (the source of the state-level data on firm sizes, employment, and sales) also occurred in that year (the Census of Manufacturing is conducted only every five years).

Results

Table A-3 presents the regression results. Overall, the regression model demonstrates considerable explanatory power. The F-statistic is significant at the one-percent confidence level, and the model explains 83 percent of the variation in pollution abatement expenditures per employee. The estimate of J3, –0.431, is significant at the 0.07 confidence level. This parameter value indicates that a 1 percent increase in firm size (the number of employees) corresponds to a 0.431 percent decrease in abatement costs per employee. (Recall that the variables are entered as log transformations, so the estimated coefficient indicates the elasticity.) The control variable for the value of sales is significant at the 0.01 level. Finally, the F-statistic allows us to reject the hypothesis that the coefficients on the industry-specific dummy variables are jointly equal to zero. In other words, not surprisingly, the fixed-effects variables pick up significant differences in costs among the various industries.

Table A-3. Regression Results: Economies of Scale in Compliance Costs: Environmental Regulations Dependent variable: Pollution Abatement Expenditure per Employee

Independent Variable	Coefficient	Std. Err.	t-stat	P>|t|
ln (Number of Employees)	-0.431	0.243	-1.78	0.07
ln (Value of Shipments)	0.698	0.186	3.75	0.00
Constant	-2.494	2.28	-1.10	0.28

Notes to Table A-3: Number of observations = 208
Adjusted R-squared = 0.83
Regression F-stat (2, 188) = 10.84
Fixed Industry Effects, F-stat (17, 188) = 18.43

Following the firm classification scheme used throughout this study, the predicted costs per employee are computed for three broad categories of firm sizes: firms with fewer than 20 employees ("small firms"), firms with 20 to 499 employees ("medium-sized firms"), and firms with 500 or more employees ("large firms"). These costs are also shown in Table A-4, converted into 2009 dollars. The relative costs across these three firm size categories for the earlier time period establish the basis for allocating the cost of environmental regulations in 2008.

Table A-4. Results on Environmental Compliance Costs by Firm Size

	(2009 Dollars)		
	Cost per Employee, Manufacturing Sector Firms with:		
	<20 Employees	20 to 499 Employees	500+ Employees
Values Using Eq. 2	22,594	7,131	4,865

Concluding Comments

The earliest studies for Advocacy (Hopkins, 1995) provided the most comprehensive assessment to date on the incidence of regulatory costs by sector and firm size. However, Hopkins pointed out, he was forced to rely on a judgmental approach to the cost allocations across firm sizes in the absence of specific empirical estimates. This appendix provides the basis used in this report (and two prior reports for Advocacy) to allocate the costs of environmental regulations among the different firm size classes.

Table A-5. Sectors Included in the Regression Analysis of Environmental Compliance Costs

SIC Code	*Industry Description*
20	Food and kindred products
21	Tobacco products
22	Textile mill products
23	Apparel and other textile products
24	Lumber and wood Products
25	Furniture and fixtures
26	Paper and allied products
27	Printing and publishing
28	Chemicals and allied products
29	Petroleum and coal products
30	Rubber and miscellaneous plastic products
31	Leather and leather products
32	Stone, clay and glass products
33	Primary metal industries
34	Fabricated metal products
35	Industrial machinery and equipment
36	Electronic and other electric equipment
37	Transportation equipment
38	Instruments and related products
39	Miscellaneous manufacturing industries

Appendix 4. Spending and Staffing by Federal Regulatory Agencies

Table A-6. Total Spending by Federal Regulatory Agencies on Regulatory Activity, Fiscal Years (Millions of 2009 Dollars)

Fiscal Year	Social Regulations	Economic Regulations	Total
1990	17,020	3,883	20,903
1991	18,588	3,736	22,323
1992	20,320	4,098	24,418
1993	20,442	4,687	25,130
1994	20,745	4,366	25,111
1995	21,243	5,076	26,319
1996	21,041	4,685	25,726
1997	22,103	5,057	27,160
1998	24,123	4,948	29,071
1999	25,034	5,197	30,231
2000	26,247	5,460	31,707
2001	27,305	5,588	32,892
2002	32,296	6,002	38,297
2003	41,683	5,926	47,609
2004	36,658	6,418	43,076
2005	36,778	6,508	43,286
2006	37,888	6,751	44,639
2007	38,267	6,988	45,256
2008	40,518	7,352	47,870

Notes to Table A-6.

Source: de Rugy and Warren (2009), Table A-5, p. 28. Their figures were derived from the Budget of the United States Government and related documents, various fiscal years.

Table A-7. Total Staffing of Federal Regulatory Activity, Fiscal Years, Full-Time Equivalent Employment

Fiscal Year	Social Regulations	Economic Regulations	Total
1990	119,459	33,155	152,614
1991	123,247	34,284	157,531
1992	130,747	36,971	167,718
1993	135,804	37,957	173,761
1994	133,487	37,499	170,986
1995	136,016	37,594	173,610
1996	136,926	33,611	170,537
1997	133,153	32,313	165,466
1998	139,794	31,848	171,642
1999	139,799	32,384	172,183
2000	143,052	32,548	175,600
2001	140,523	32,270	172,793
2002	152,585	32,436	185,021
2003	210,316	31,981	242,297
2004	202,195	32,559	234,754
2005	203,417	32,312	235,729
2006	201,961	32,567	234,528
2007	204,893	33,440	238,333
2008	215,147	34,324	249,471

Notes to Table A-7. Source: de Rugy and Warren (2009), Table A-6, p. 29. Their figures were derived from the Budget of the United States Government and related documents, various fiscal years.

BIBLIOGRAPHY

Anderson, P.M. and Meyer, B.D. (1997). The effects of firm specific taxes and government mandates with an application to the U.S. unemployment insurance program. *Journal of Public Economics,* 65, 119-45.

Antonelli, Angela. (1995). *The U.S. Paperwork Reduction Act after fifteen years.* (PUMA/REG(95)4).Paris: Organisation for Economic Cooperation and Development.

Arnold, F. (1995). *Economic analysis of environmental policy and regulation.* New York: John Wiley and Sons.

Barro, Robert J. (1997). *Determinants of economic growth: A cross-country empirical study.* Cambridge, MA: MIT Press.

Barro, Robert J. and Sala-i-Martin, X. (1995). *Economic growth.* New York: McGraw-Hill.

Becker, Randy A. (2005). Air pollution abatement costs under the Clean Air Act: Evidence from the PACE survey. *Journal of Environmental Economics and Management,* 5, 144-169.

Bradford, Steven C. (2004). Does size matter? An economic analysis of small business exemptions from regulation. *The Journal of Small and Emerging Business Law,* 8 (1), 1-37.

Byars, John D., McCormick, Robert E., and Yandle, T. Bruce. (1999). *Economic freedom in America's 50 states: A 1999 analysis.* Clemson, SC: Clemson University, State Policy Network.

Cole, Roland J. and Sommers, Paul. (1980). *Costs of compliance in small and moderate- sized businesses*. (SBA-79-2668). Seattle, WA: Battelle Human Affairs Research Centers.

Crain, W. Mark.(2005). *The impact of regulatory costs on small firms*, Washington, DC: U.S. Small Business Administration, Office of Advocacy. (http://www.sba.gov/advo/).

Crain, W. Mark and Hopkins, Thomas D. (2001). *The impact of regulatory costs on small firms.* Washington, DC: U.S. Small Business Administration, Office of Advocacy. (http://www.sba.gov/advo/).

Crain, W. Mark and Johnson, Joseph. (2001). *Compliance costs of federal workplace regulations: Survey results for U.S. manufacturers. (*Working paper). Arlington, VA: George Mason University, Mercatus Center.

Crain, W. Mark. (2010). *18 million words can hurt you: The cost of state environmental regulations.* (Policy Studies Working Paper). Easton, PA: Lafayette College.

Crews, Jr., Clyde Wayne. (2004). *Ten thousand commandments: An annual snapshot of the federal regulatory state.* Washington, DC: Cato Institute.

de Rugy, Veronique and Warren, Melinda. (2009). *Expansion of regulatory budgets and staffing continues to rise: An analysis of the U.S. budget for fiscal years 2009 and 2010. (*Regulatory Report 31). Arlington, VA: George Mason University, Mercatus Center.

Dean, Thomas J. (1994). *Pollution regulations as a barrier to the formation of small manufacturing establishments: A longitudinal analysis.* Washington, DC: U.S. Small Business Administration, Office of Advocacy.

Dean, T. J., Brown, R.L., and Stango, V. (2000). Environmental regulation as a barrier to the formation of small manufacturing establishments: A longitudinal analysis. *Journal of Environmental Economics and Management,* 40, 56-75.

Donez, F. (1997). *Environmental regulations and small manufacturing plants: Evidence from three industries.* (Unpublished manuscript). Washington, DC: U.S. Environmental Protection Agency, Office of Policy.

Dudley, Susan E. and Antonelli, Angela. (1997). Congress and the Clinton OMB: Unwilling partners in regulatory oversight. *Regulation.*

Evans, Donald S. (1985). *An analysis of the differential impact of EPA and OSHA regulations across firm and establishment size in the manufacturing industries.*Washington, DC: U.S. Small Business Administration, Office of Advocacy.

Executive Order 12866 (1993). Regulatory Planning and Review. *Federal Register*, 58 FR 51735. (http://www.epa.gov/fedrgstr/eo/eo12866.htm).

Friedman, Milton. (2009, January 15). What every American wants. *Wall Street Journal*, A10.

Gruber, Jonathon. (2004). *Public finance and public policy*. New York: Worth Publishers.

Hahn, Robert W. and Hird, John A. (1991). The costs and benefits of regulation: Review and synthesis. *Yale Journal of Regulation,* 8(1), 233-278.

Hahn, Robert W. (1996). Regulatory reform: What do the government's numbers tell us? In Robert W. Hahn (Ed.), *Risks, costs, and lives saved: Getting better results from regulation* (pp. 208-253). New York: Oxford University Press and AEI Press.

Hahn, Robert W. (1998). Government analysis of the benefits and costs of regulation. *Journal of Economic Perspectives*, 12 (4), 201-210.

Hahn, Robert W. (2001). Regulatory reform: Assessing the government's numbers. In *Reviving regulatory reform: A global perspective.* New York: Cambridge University Press and AEI Press.

Hall, J. V. (1997). The theoretical and empirical basis for assessing economic impacts of environmental regulation. In D. C. Hall (Ed.), *Advances in the economics of environmental resources* (pp. 13-37). New York: JAI Press, Inc.

Hall, Robert E. and Jones, Charles I. (1997). Levels of economic activity across countries. *American Economic Review*, 87 (2), 173-177.

Harrington, Winston, Morgenstern, Richard D., and Nelson, Peter. (2000). On the accuracy of regulatory cost estimates. *Journal of Policy Analysis and Management*, 19 (2), 297-322.

Hazilla, Michael and Kopp, Raymond. (1990). The social cost of environmental quality regulations: A general equilibrium analysis. *Journal of Political Economy*, 98 (4), 853-873.

Hopkins, T. D. (1995). *A survey of regulatory burdens.* (Report no.SBA-8029-OA-93).

Washington, DC: U.S. Small Business Administration, Office of Advocacy. (http://www.sba.gov/advo/research/rs163.html).

Hopkins, Thomas. (1995). *Profiles of regulatory costs. Report to the U.S. Small Business Administration.* (NTIS No.PB96 128038). Washington, DC: U. S. Small Business Administration, Office of Advocacy. (http://www.sba.gov/advo/).

Huang, Ying, McCormick, Robert E., and McQuillen, Lawrence. (2004). *U.S. Economic Freedom Index: 2004 report.* San Francisco: Pacific Research Institute.

Jaffe, Adam B., Peterson, Steven R., Portney, Paul R., and Stavins, Robert. (1995). Environmental regulation and the competitiveness of U.S. manufacturing. *Journal of Economic Literature*, 33 (1), 132-163.

James, Jr., Harvey S. (1996). Estimating OSHA compliance costs. (Policy Study no. 135). St. Louis: Washington University, Center for the Study of American Business.

Johnson, Joseph M. (2004). *The cost of regulations implementing the Clean Water Act.* (Regulatory Studies Program working paper). Arlington, VA: George Mason University, Mercatus Center.

Johnson, Joseph M. (2005) A review and synthesis of the cost of workplace regulations. In Andrew P. Morriss and Samuel Estreicher (Eds.), *Cross-border human resources, labor and employment issues* (pp. 433-467). Netherlands: Kluwer Law International.

Jorgenson, Dale W. and Wilcoxen, Peter J. (1990). Environmental regulation and U.S. economic growth. *Rand Journal of Economics,* 21 (2), 314-340.

Julien, P.A. (1993). Small businesses as a research subject: Some reflections on knowledge of small businesses and its effects on economic theory. *Small Business Economics,* 5, 157-166.

Karabegovic, Amela and McMahon, Fred, with Black, Christy G. (Annual editions, 2002-2009). *Economic freedom of North America.* Canada: The Fraser Institute.

Kaufmann, Daniel and Kraay, Aart. (2008, spring). Governance indicators: Where are we and where should we be going? *World Bank Research Observer.*

Kaufmann, Daniel, Kraay, Aart, and Mastruzzi, Massimo. (2009, June). Governance matters VIII: Aggregate and individual governance indicators 1996–2008. (Policy Research Working Paper 4978). Washington, DC:

World Bank Development Research Group, Macroeconomics and Growth Team.

Kirchhoff, B. A. and Greene, P.G. (1996). Understanding the theoretical and empirical content of critiques of U.S. job creation. *Small Business Economics,* 10, 153-169.

Kohn, R. E. (1988). Efficient scale of the pollution-abating firm. *Land Economics,* 64(1), 53-61.

List, John and Kunce, Mitch. (2000). Environmental protection and economic growth: What do the residuals tell us? *Land Economics*, *76*(2), 267-282.

McQuillan, Lawrence J., Maloney, Michael T., Daniels, Eric, and Eastwood, Brent M. (2008). *U.S. Economic Freedom Index: 2008 report.* San Francisco: Pacific Research Institute.

Madrian, B. C. (1998, winter). Health insurance portability: The consequences of COBRA. *Regulation,* 27-33.

Martin, S. (1993). *Advanced industrial economics.* Cambridge, MA: Blackwell.

Moody, J. Scott. (2000). *The cost of complying with the U.S. federal income tax*. Washington, DC: The Tax Foundation.

Moody, J. Scott. (2002). *The cost of complying with the U.S. federal income tax* Washington, DC: The Tax Foundation.

Morrison, Todd A. (1984). *Economies of scale in regulatory compliance: Evidence of the differential impacts of regulation by firm size*. (Jack Faucett Associates.) Washington, DC: U.S. Small Business Administration, Office of Advocacy. (NTIS no. PB85-178861),

Organisation for Economic Cooperation and Development. (1997). *The OECD report on regulatory reform. Volume I: Sectoral studies.* Paris: Author.

Organisation for Economic Cooperation and Development. (1999a). *Regulatory reform in the United State*s. (OECD Reviews of Regulatory Reform). Paris: Author.

Organisation for Economic Cooperation and Development. (1999b). Cross-country patterns of product market regulation. *Economic outlook,*Chapter VII (pp. 179- 189). Paris: Author.

Organisation for Economic Cooperation and Development. (2000). *Summary indicators of product market regulation with an extension to employment protection legislation.* (Economics Department Working Paper No. 226). Paris: Author.

National Federation of Independent Business Education Foundation. (2000). William J. Dennis, Jr. (Ed.), *NFIB small business policy guide.*

Washington, DC: Author. (http://www.nfib.com/PDFs/NFIBPolicy Guide.pdf).

Nicoletti, G., Scarpetta, S., and Boylaud, O. (1999). *Summary indicators of product market regulation and employment protection legislation for the purpose of international*

comparisons. (OECD Economics Department Working Paper No. 226).Paris: Organisation for Economic Cooperation and Development.

Oats, Wallace. (2009, September 21). *Environmental federalism.* Washington, DC: Resources for the Future.

Pashigian, B. P. (1984). The effect of environmental regulation on optimal plant size and factor shares. *Journal of Law and Economics*, 27, 1-28.

Pashigian, B. P. (1986). Reply to Evans. *Journal of Law and Economics,* 29, 201-209.

Phillips, Bruce D. and Dennis, Jr., William J. (2001, May 21). *Better measures of regulatory costs as support for entrepreneurship.* (Mimeograph). Washington. DC: National Federation of Independent Business Educational Foundation.

Pittman, R. W. (1981). Issue in pollution control: Interplant cost differences and economies of scale. *Land Economics,* 57(1), 1-14.

Porter, Michael. (1991). America's green strategy. *Scientific American*.

Posner, Richard A. (1975). The social costs of monopoly and regulation. *Journal of Political Economy*, 83(4), 807-828.

Potter, E. E. and Reesman, A.E. (1990). An assessment of remedies: The impact of compensatory and punitive damages on Title VII. (Policy paper). Washington, DC: Employment Policy Foundation.

Regulatory Flexibility Act. (1980). 5 U.S.C. Section 605.

Sargentich, T. O. (1997). The Small Business Regulatory Enforcement Fairness Act. *Administrative Law Review,* 49 (1), 123-138.

Schmalensee, Richard. (1994). The costs of environmental protection. In M.B. Kotowski (Ed.), *Balancing economic growth and environmental goals* (pp. 57-61). Washington, DC: American Council for Capital Formation.

Siegfried, J. J. and Evans, l.B. (1994). Empirical studies of entry and exit: A survey of the evidence. *Review of Industrial Organization,* 9, 121-155.

Staley, Samuel R., Husock, Howard, Bobb, David J., Burnett, Sterling, Crasy, Laura, and Hudson, Wade. (2001). *Giving a leg up to bootstrap entrepreneurship: Expanding economic opportunity In America's urban centers.* Los Angeles, CA: Reason Public Policy Institute.

Storey, D. J. (1994). *Understanding the small business sector.* London: Routledge.

Thieblot, A.J. (1996). A new evaluation of impacts of prevailing wage law repeal. *Journal of Labor Research,* 17(2), 297-322.

U.S. Bureau of the Census. (1992). Economic Census (http://govinfo.kerr. orst.edu/econstateis.html).

U.S. Bureau of the Census, Bureau of Economic Analysis. (1996). Pollution abatement and control expenditures, 1972–94. *Survey of Current Business*, 76.

U.S. Bureau of Labor Statistics. (2001). Labor force statistics from the Current Population Survey. (http://stats.bls.gov/news.release/union2.t03.htm).

U.S. Department of Health and Human Services. (2009). *National health expenditure accounts.* Washington, DC: Author. (http://www.cms.hhs.gov /NationalHealthExpendData/02_NationalHealthAccounts_Historical. asp# TopOfPage).

U.S. Environmental Protection Agency. (1990). *Environmental investments: The cost of a clean environment.* (EPA 230-11-90-083). Washington, DC: Author.

U.S. Environmental Protection Agency. (1999a). *Economic analysis of the proposed boat manufacturing NESHAP.* (EPA-452/R). Washington, DC: Author.

U.S. Environmental Protection Agency. (1999b). *Revised interim guidance for rulewriters: Regulatory Flexibility Act as amended by the Small Business Regulatory Enforcement Fairness Act.* Washington, DC: Author. (www.EPA.Gov/SBREFA)

U.S. Environmental Protection Agency. (2000). *A retrospective assessment of the costs of the Clean Water Act: 1972 to 1997.* Washington, DC: Author.

U.S. General Accounting Office. (1994). *Workplace regulation.*Vol. 1 (GAO/HEHS-94- 138). Washington, DC: Author.

U.S. International Trade Commission. (2004). *The economic effects of significant U.S. import restraints.* Fourth update. (Investigation No. 332-325). Washington, DC: Author.

U.S. Office of Management and Budget, Office of Information and Regulatory Affairs. (2000). *Report to Congress on the costs and benefits of federal regulations.* Washington, DC: Author.

U.S. Office of Management and Budget, Office of Information and Regulatory Affairs. (2001). *Report to Congress on the costs and benefits of federal regulations.* Washington, DC: Author.

U.S. Office of Management and Budget, Office of Information and Regulatory Affairs. (2002). *Informing regulatory decisions: Report to Congress on the costs and benefits of federal regulations.* Washington, DC: Author.

U.S. Office of Management and Budget, Office of Information and Regulatory Affairs. (2003). *Informing regulatory decisions: Report to Congress on the costs and benefits of federal regulations*. Washington, DC: Author.

U.S. Office of Management and Budget, Office of Information and Regulatory Affairs. (2004). *Informing regulatory decisions: 2004 draft report to Congress on the costs and benefits of federal regulations*. Washington, DC: Author.

U.S. Office of Management and Budget, Office of Information and Regulatory Affairs. (2005). *Draft report to Congress on the costs and benefits of federal regulations*. Washington, DC: Author.

U.S. Small Business Administration. (1998a). Impacts of federal regulations, paperwork, and tax requirements on small business. (SBAHQ-95-C-0023) Washington, DC: Author. (http://www.sba.gov/ADVO/research/# regulation).

U.S. Small Business Administration. (1998b). Small business answer card. Washington, DC: Author. (http://www.sba.gov/advo/stats/ec_anscd.html).

U.S. Small Business Administration, Office of Advocacy. (2001). Statistics of businesses: Firm size data. Washington, DC: Author. (http://www.sba. gov/advo/stats/data.html).

U.S. Small Business Administration, Office of Advocacy. (Annual editions). *Annual report of the chief counsel for advocacy on implementation of the Regulatory Flexibility Act and Executive Order 13272*. Washington, DC: Author. (http://www.sba.gov/advo/laws/flex/).

Varshney, Sanjay B. and Tootelian, Daniel H. (2009). *Cost of state regulations on California small businesses study*. Sacramento, CA: California State University.

Verkuil, P. R. (1982). A critical guide to the Regulatory Flexibility Act. *Duke Law Journal,* 213-275.

Walker, Deborah. (1988). Mandatory family-leave legislation: The hidden costs. *Policy Analysis*, No. 108.

Warren, Melinda. (2000, June). *Federal regulatory spending reaches a new height: An analysis of the budget of the U.S. government for the year 2001.* (Regulatory

Report No. 23). St. Louis: Washington University, Center for the Study of American Business.(http://csab.wustl.edu/New%20WC%20Site/CSAB%20publications/CSAB%20pu bs-pdf%20files/RBR/RBR%2023.pdf)

Winston, Clifford. (1998). U.S. industry adjustment to economic deregulation. *Journal of Economic Perspectives,* 12(3), 89-110.

Wittenberg, A. and Arnold, F. (1999). *Review of small entity economic impact analysis*. (Unpublished manuscript prepared by ICF Consulting for U.S. Environmental Protection Agency, Contract 68-W6-0056).

End Notes

[1] Section 624 of the Treasury and General Government Appropriations Act of 2001, Pub. L. 106-554, 31 U.S.C. § 1105 note.

[2] Thomas D. Hopkins, *Profiles of Regulatory Costs. Report to the U.S. Small Business Administration*, U.S. Department of Commerce, National Technical Information Service #PB96 128038, November 1995 (http://www.sba.gov/advo/). W. Mark Crain and Thomas D. Hopkins, *The Impact of Regulatory Costs on Small Firms*, U.S. Small Business Administration, 2001 (http://www.sba.gov/advo/). Hopkins (1995) began to fill the information vacuum regarding the federal regulatory burden, presenting a profile of the level and distribution of federal regulatory compliance costs using data through 1992, and made cost projections through 2000. The Hopkins study was updated and extended in Crain and Hopkins (2001); that study examined the actual, as distinct from projected, regulatory burden in 2000. Crain (2005) updated and provided methodological revisions to the 2001 study and estimated compliance costs for 2004.

[3] U.S. Office of Management and Budget, Office of Information and Regulatory Affairs (2005), *Draft Report to Congress on the Costs and Benefits of Federal Regulations*, p. 9.

[4] In some cases, the cost estimates are based on OMB's transparent modifications of agency-provided cost-benefit estimates. Agencies are not required to perform cost-benefit analyses on regulations that are expected to have an economic impact of less than $100 million, and thus these are omitted from OMB's cost estimate.

[5] For example, regulations implemented directly through the legislative process are outside the OMB review process. Furthermore, the totality of rules, both existing and new, with anticipated impacts below $100 million, and not subject to the Paperwork Reduction Act, are also outside the OMB review process.

[6] Exec. Order No. 12,866 §1(a), 58 Fed. Reg. 51,735 (Sept. 30, 1993).

[7] On this subject, OMB (2009, p. 23) states that "...it would be highly desirable to obtain better information on the costs and benefits of these rules." The OMB reports provide in tabular form information that is available from the Government Accountability Office (GAO) about the costs and benefits of regulations issued by independent regulatory agencies. As OMB (2009) notes, monetized costs were reported for only two rules issued by independent regulatory agencies for the period 2007-2008.

[8] Tables 7 and 8 provide snapshots of the size distribution of American businesses. It should be pointed out that large firms employ 50 percent of all workers, whereas small firms employ 18 percent of all workers in the United States. These snapshots are computed from data compiled by the U.S. Census Bureau for Advocacy (source: U.S. Small Business Administration website, http://www.sba.gov/advo/research/data.html). For general information about the relevance of small business to the US economy, see Frequently Asked Questions on the U.S. SBA website, http://web.sba.gov/faqs/faqindex.cfm?areaID=24.

9 Milton Friedman put the estimated burden of government mandates and regulations at roughly 10 percent of U.S. national income in 2003. See Milton Friedman, "What Every American Wants," *Wall Street Journal,* January 15, 2003, p. A10.

10 Studies on the incidence of regulatory costs among firms of different sizes include Henry B. R. Beale and King Lin, *Impacts of Federal Regulations, Paperwork, and Tax Requirements on Small Business*, SBAHQ-95-C-0023; Microeconomic Applications, Inc., prepared for the Office of Advocacy, U.S. Small Business Administration, September 1998; Roland J. Cole and Paul Sommers, *Costs of Compliance in Small and Moderate-sized Businesses*, SBA-79-2668, Battelle Human Affairs Research Centers, Seattle, WA, February 1980; *Improving Economic Analysis of Government Regulations on Small Business*, SBA-2648-OA-79, JACA Corporation, Fort Washington, PA, January 1981; Robert J. Gaston and Sidney L. Carroll, *State and Local Regulatory Restrictions as Fixed Cost Barriers to Small Business Enterprise*, SBA-7167-AER-83, Applied Economics Group, Inc., Knoxville, TN, April 1984; and, *Economies of Scale in Regulatory Compliance: Evidence of the Differential Impacts of Regulation by Firm Size*, SBA-7188-OA-83, Jack Faucett Associates, Chevy Chase, MD, December 1984. For a theoretical discussion, see William A. Brock and David S. Evans, *The Economics of Small Businesses: Their Role and Regulation in the U.S. Economy*, Holmes and Meier, New York, NY, 1986, especially chapters 4 and 5. A recent survey and extension of this literature is provided by Steven C. Bradford, "Does Size Matter? An Economic Analysis of Small Business Exemptions from Regulation," *The Journal of Small and Emerging Business Law,* 8 (1), 2004, pp. 1-37.

11 This may be especially relevant in the cost of complying with Section 404 of the Sarbanes-Oxley Act of 2002. The impact of the exemption of small business entities has resulted in cost savings in the billions. See U.S. Small Business Administration, Office of Advocacy (annual editions), *Annual Report of the Chief Counsel for Advocacy on Implementation of the Regulatory Flexibility Act and Executive Order 13272.*

12 The "other" category includes the following industries: forestry, fishing, hunting and agriculture; mining; utilities; construction; and transportation and warehousing.

13 These data are from Veronique de Rugy and Melinda Warren (2009), *Expansion of Regulatory' Budgets and Staffing Continues to Rise: An Analysis of the U.S. Budget for Fiscal Years 2009 and 2010,* Regulatory Report 31, Arlington, VA: Mercatus Center, George Mason University. Appendix 4 in this report presents additional data from their study of regulatory budgets and staffing.

14 See W.M. Crain, "18 Millions Words Can Hurt You: The Cost of State Environmental Regulations," Policy Studies Working Paper, Lafayette College, 2010.

15 A recent study of California state regulations estimated the costs of that state's regulation to be $493 billion in 2007; see Sanjay B. Varshney, and Daniel H. Tootelian, *Cost of State Regulations on California Small Businesses Study,* California State University, Sacramento, September 2009. Other researchers have ranked states in terms of their relative regulatory burden, for examples: John D. Byars, Robert E. McCormick, and T. Bruce Yandle, *Economic Freedom in America's 50 States: A 1999 Analysis*, State Policy Network, 1999; Ying Huang, Robert E. McCormick, and Lawrence McQuillen, *U.S. Economic Freedom Index: 2004 Report*, Pacific Research Institute, 2004; and Lawrence J. McQuillan, Michael T. Maloney, Eric Daniels, and Brent M. Eastwood, *U.S. Economic Freedom Index: 2008 Report,* Pacific Research Institute, 2008. A different methodology is used by Amela Karabegovic and Fred McMahon (with Christy G. Black) to rank American States and Canadian Provinces. See *Economic Freedom of North* America, The Fraser Institute, annual

editions since 2002. No estimates seem to be available for the aggregate costs of state regulations for the 50 states.

16 The effect of regulations on dynamic efficiency is not without opposing viewpoints. Perhaps the most famous is Professor Porter's theory that environmental progress and economic competitiveness are not inconsistent but complementary, See Michael Porter, "America's Green Strategy," *Scientific American* (1991), For a critique of the Porter theory, see for examples, Oats, Wallace, "Environmental Federalism," Washington, DC: Resources for the Future, Sept. 21, 2009; and John List and Mitch Kunce, "Environmental Protection and Economic Growth: What Do the Residuals Tell Us?, *Land Economics*, 2000, *76*(2), pp. 267-82.

17 The effects of regulations on economic growth are recognized and discussed by OMB in its annual reports to Congress, but are not included in its cost estimates. The study by Hazilla and Kopp estimates of the indirect effects of environmental regulations as well as the dynamic consequences. Their evidence suggests that both of these costs are substantial. See Michael Hazilla and Raymond Kopp, "The Social Cost of Environmental Quality Regulations: A General Equilibrium Analysis," *Journal of Political Economy*, Vol. 98 (4), 1990. It is important to emphasize that the benefits of regulations might also be greater in a general equilibrium analysis than in partial equilibrium, and thus social welfare (benefits net of costs) might be higher in a general equilibrium than in a partial equilibrium analysis.

18 These four categories differ slightly from those used in Crain (2005) and Crain and Hopkins (2001). They continue to conform reasonably well with the categories used by the U.S. Office of Management and Budget in its annual reports to Congress. Hopkins (1995) used slightly different categories: environmental, other social, economic, and process. Occupational health and safety regulations and homeland security regulations are combined on the rationale that both deal broadly with public safety issues.

19 Under Executive Order 12866, OMB requires and reviews regulations issued by executive branch agencies. This means, for example, that the costs are not included for rules issued by such agencies as: the Securities and Exchange Commission, the Consumer Product Safety Commission, the Federal Communications Commission, the Federal Trade Commission, and the Nuclear Regulatory Commission. The U.S. Government Accountability Office (GAO) is required by statute to report to Congress on major regulatory rules, including those issued by agencies not subject to Executive Order 12866. This GAO report, however, still does not include cost estimates for most federal regulations.

20 It is interesting to note that in its 2000 Report to Congress, OMB used a comparable methodology and OECD data to include a more expansive estimate of the costs of economic regulations than it used in subsequent Reports to Congress. A similar regression methodology is employed by Varshney and Tootelian, *op. cit.*, to estimate the cost of state-level regulations in California. They use indices that gauge the extent of state government regulations and analyze the impact on gross state product, controlling for various factors that influence state economic performance.

21 A detailed description of the methodology used in its construction is provided in Daniel Kaufmann, Aart Kraay, and Massimo Mastruzzi, "Governance Matters VIII: Aggregate and Individual Governance Indicators 1996–2008," World Bank Development Research Group, Macroeconomics and Growth Team, Policy Research Working Paper 4978, June 2009. See especially Appendix D. For further discussion of applications of the governance metrics see Kaufmann, Daniel and Aart Kraay (2008). "Governance Indicators: Where Are We and Where Should We Be Going?" *World Bank Research Observer*, Spring 2008. As noted in the text, the prior study (Crain, 2005) introduced this methodological approach as a baseline

estimate for economic regulations, except that it used an index of regulations compiled by researchers at the Organization for Economic Cooperation and Development. (See G. Nicoletti, Scarpetta and O. Boylaud (2000), "Summary Indicators of Product Market Regulation and Employment Protection Legislation for the Purpose of International Comparisons," *OECD Economics Department Working Paper*, No. 226.) It is noteworthy that the OECD and WGI indices are correlated over the time periods for which both indices are available. The WGI index is employed in this report because it is available annually for a longer and more recent time period, while the OECD index is only available at five-year intervals: 1998, 2003, and 2008. Prior studies by Crain and Hopkins (2001) and OMB (2000) used an estimate based on the OECD findings in *Regulatory Reform in the United States*, OECD Reviews of Regulatory Reform, Paris, 1999. One criticism of the earlier method is that it fails to account adequately for major deregulation activities in various industries in the 1980s and 1990s.

[22] The OECD Index used in Crain (2005) was based on the OECD Survey for 1998. Criticism of the short time period is raised in Winston Harrington, "Grading Estimates of the Benefits and Costs of Federal Regulation: A Review of Reviews," RFF Discussion Paper 06-39, Washington, DC: Resources for the Future. September 2006. See especially pages 14-16. Of course, a larger sample size generally improves the reliability of statistical estimation.

[23] Values for the Regulatory Quality Index are available for many OECD countries starting in 1996. The sample in the regression model includes seven years, 2002 through 2008. This is because data for some of the control variables used to estimate Equation (1) are missing for various countries before 2002. Thus, the sample of countries that may be used in the analysis increases to 25 by beginning the sample in 2002.

[24] For comparison, when Equation (1) is estimated without the country fixed-effects variables, the estimated coefficient on the *World Bank Regulatory Quality Index* equals 0.142, which is significant at the 1 percent confidence level. In other words, the parameter estimate used in the report for the cost of economic regulations is on the low end of the range of estimates using this regression analysis.

[25] It is worth reiterating that OMB includes only the costs of "economically significant" regulations subject to E.O. 12866 review. These are less than 1 percent of EPA's rulemaking. Moreover, as noted earlier, the OMB annual reports now encompass only regulations issued in the prior 10 years. This was not always the case, and data on the earlier environmental regulations are summarized in OMB's past annual reports

[26] U.S. Office of Management and Budget, Office of Information and Regulatory Affairs (2003), *Informing Regulatory Decisions: Report to Congress on the Costs and Benefits of Federal Regulations*, Table 2. OMB's cost estimates rely on regulatory impact analyses (RIAs) issued mainly by the U.S. Environmental Protection Agency.

[27] Several regulatory experts draw a similar conclusion about the OMB environmental cost estimates, but considerable debate continues. For example, Johnson concludes that "the costs of water quality regulation totaled $93.1 billion in 2001. While this figure is based on conservative estimates of regulatory costs, it is significantly larger than the cost and benefit estimates produced by EPA." (Joseph Johnson, *The Cost of Regulations Implementing the Clean Water Act,* Arlington, VA: Mercatus Center, Regulatory Studies Program Working Paper, April 2004.) In contrast, in 1999, EPA estimated the costs of the 1972 Clean Water Act at $15.8 billion per year. ("A Retrospective Assessment of the Costs of the Clean Water Act: 1972 to 1997," U.S. Environmental Protection Agency, October 2000.) The discussion in Robert W. Hahn, "Regulatory Reform: What Do the Government's Numbers Tell Us?" in Robert W. Hahn (ed.) *Risks, Costs, and Lives Saved: Getting Better Results from*

Regulation, New York: Oxford University Press and AEI Press, 1996, pp. 208-253, is also informative. Hahn makes a strong case that government agencies overestimate benefits and underestimate costs systematically. In addition, the review article by Jaffe, *et al.*, "Environmental Regulation and the Competitiveness of U.S. Manufacturing," *Journal of Economic Literature*, Vol. 33 (1), 1995, suggests that environmental costs in the long run have exceeded compliance cost estimates. Finally, the study by Winston Harrington, *et al.* "On the Accuracy of Regulatory Cost Estimates," *Journal of Policy Analysis and Management*, vol. 19 (2), 2000, examines the estimates for 28 particular rules promulgated by EPA and OSHA and finds, in contrast, that overestimation of unit costs occurs about as often as underestimation.

[28] The source of the hourly rate data is the U.S. Bureau of Labor Statistics website.

[29] The source for the cost estimate for workplace regulations is the 2005 study by Joseph Johnson. The Johnson study offers a synthesis and evaluation of available estimates of the cost of regulations directed at the workplace, and from these different studies, generates an estimate of the total cost of workplace regulation. It provides the most comprehensive analysis to date, covering the 25 statutory acts and executive orders that encompass all significant workplace regulations promulgated by the federal government through 2001. Joseph M. Johnson, "A Review and Synthesis of the Cost of Workplace Regulations," in *Cross-Border Human Resources, Labor and Employment Issues*. Andrew P. Morriss and Samuel Estreicher (eds.), Kluwer Law International: Netherlands, 2005, pp. 433-67.

[30] The U.S. Census Bureau provides Advocacy with these data. The Statistics of U.S. Business covers almost all nonfarm employer businesses. It omits farms, railroads, and most government-owned establishments, the U.S. Postal Service, and large pension, health, and welfare funds (100 + employees) and nonincorporated firms with no paid employees. According to the Census Bureau, nonemployers account for roughly 3 percent of all business activity (see U.S. Census Bureau, "Nonemployer Statistics," http://www.census.gov/epcd/nonemployer).

[31] American industry is obviously not static and these 2006 data on the distribution of business activity do not match up exactly with the years for the regulatory cost data. However, changes in the basic structure of American industry generally occur only incrementally. These data provide a reasonable approximation for the relevant years of the proportions of firms, employees, and payroll across the three firm size categories and the five sector classifications.

[32] The Office of Advocacy of the U.S. Small Business Administration contracts with the U.S. Census Bureau to collect the employer firm size data (see http://www.sba.gov/advo/stats/data.html). When the Census Bureau compiles its *Statistics of U.S. Businesses*, it relies on survey questionnaires filled out by firms. Occasionally, firms classify themselves under more than one industry type (or NAICS classification). This means that when summed by sector, the number of firms is greater than the actual number of firms. The data used in this report are corrected for this over count using a technique explained in Appendix 4. In brief, the correction relies on the fact that the number of employees in each industry is accurately reported to the Census Bureau, and the share of employees by sector is used to eliminate the redundancy and scale back over counts of firms.

[33] Environmental Protection Agency, "Environmental Investments: The Cost of a Clean Environment," EPA 230-11-90-083, November 1990, pp. 2-5.

[34] Moreover, this assumption is similar to that used by the Congressional Budget Office that payroll taxes are borne fully by workers (and therefore not shifted forward onto consumers

through price increases). See the discussion in Jonathon Gruber, *Public Finance and Public Policy*, New York: Worth Publishers, 2004, pp. 539-540.

[35] The NAICS data are from the U.S. Census Bureau website: http://www.census.gov/epcd/naics 02/naicod02.htm

[36] The source of the value added to GDP by sector and the private sector GDP data is the Industry Economics Division, Bureau of Economic Analysis (BEA), U.S. Department of Commerce. The data used were released on April 28, 2009. The source for the employment data is U.S. Small Business Administration, Office of Advocacy, "Statistics of U.S. Businesses: Firm Size Data," website: http://www.sba.gov/advo/stats/data.html.

[37] Michael Hazilla and Raymond Kopp (1990), "The Social Cost of Environmental Quality Regulations: A General Equilibrium Analysis," *Journal of Political Economy*, Vol. 98 (4), p. 858.

[38] See, for examples, Thomas J. Dean, *Pollution Regulations as a Barrier to the Formation of Small Manufacturing Establishments: A Longitudinal Analysis*, Office of Advocacy, U.S. Small Business Administration: Washington, D.C., 1994; and Thomas J. Dean, *et al.*, "Environmental Regulation as a Barrier to the Formation of Small Manufacturing Establishments: A Longitudinal Analysis," *Journal of Environmental Economics and Management* 40, 2000, pp. 56-75. These two studies suggest that regulatory costs lower the startup rate for new firms, especially in the manufacturing sector, because of its higher capital requirements from environmental and other types of regulations. They also indicate that environmental regulations increase the minimum efficient scale of production. See also the related study by Samuel Staley, *et al.*, *Giving A Leg Up to Bootstrap Entrepreneurship: Expanding Economic Opportunity in America's Urban Centers*, Los Angeles: Reason Public Policy Institute, 2001. As noted in the text, a recent student finds that relative costs of pollution abatement by firm size vary depending on the type of regulated pollutant. See Randy A. Becker, "Air Pollution Abatement Costs under the Clean Air Act: Evidence from the PACE Survey," *Journal of Environmental Economics and Management*, (5) 2005, pp. 144-169.

[39] The category of workplace regulations is the one area that applies this judgmental cost allocation used in Hopkins (1995), Crain and Hopkins (2001), and Crain (2005). That is, the 20 percent assumption is applied solely to a relatively small segment of all regulations, and therefore the overall results are not very sensitive to this assumption.

[40] The U.S. total figures are based on a weighted average of the costs in the five business categories. The weights for each average use the share for the respective category. For example, for the "cost per firm" value, the cost per firm in each sector is weighted by the share of all U.S. firms in that sector. For the "cost as a percent of payroll" value, the sector values are weighted by the share of all U.S. payroll expenditures in that sector, and so on.

[41] The caution about comparing the 2008 estimates with prior years again should be noted because of the newly introduced methodology for estimating economic regulations.

[42] The relatively large impact of economic regulations on large firms has been noted by a number of scholars. See the literature review in Steven C. Bradford, "Does Size Matter? An Economic Analysis of Small Business Exemptions from Regulation," *The Journal of Small and Emerging Business Law,* 8 (1), 2004, pp. 1-37.

INDEX

A

B

C

D

E

F

G

M

N

O

P

T

U

V

W

Y